This collection of happenings on the roads of my running life are merely offered for your entertainment and to help you define what running may mean to you in your life. At the end of each mile is the lesson that experience taught me. Good luck, reading, running, learning, and defining what running means to you.

I have attempted to obtain permission for everything found in this work and to give proper acknowledgement for anything that is not original. A lifetime of running, racing, reading and coaching gets complicated, and I am not sure where every quote and running statement originated. If through inadvertence a copyright has not been acknowledged, sincere apologies are offered with the assurance that this omission will be corrected in any future additions.

Cover photo provided by and used by permission of skinnyski. com. Other photos are taken by the author or used with permission from the photo company indicated.

Editing services provided by Charlotte Juaire. I thank her for her patience, cooperation and diligence in seeing me through this project.

Copyright 2011 by Dennis Bartz

Printed by Richards Publishing, Gonvick, MN

ISBN: 978-0-9759180-5-0

"I ran six miles today. I am 57 years old, the temperature was 33 degrees, the run was slow, but very good. It is the last day of November, 2010, and I am getting at the finalization of this running book. I have had thousands of runs like today's, some shorter, some longer, some faster, some more intense, but all experiencing life on the run. It is my extreme desire to attempt to share with you some of what running has given to me…"

FAVORITE MILE MARKERS

STRETCHING

It was an early northern Minnesota morning, sunny, fresh, and cool, when the air is so pleasant a person can't help just pulling it into their lungs and letting a smile land on their face. I was covered with sweat. The tree-canopied gravel road had been my friend that day. It kept my sweating mechanism working so all of my running muscles were thoroughly warm, allowing for a steady pace crusin' on the run and it felt just perfect. We had started over an hour and a half earlier, one of those unknown running routes, plenty of rolling hills, an out and back route, and it was simply where I was meant to be. Others who attended the workshop were probably still dreaming in the sheets, sleeping off the party the night before, eating breakfast, or having a quiet moment down by the lake. Not us. We were out in the middle of nowhere, a former football player, a guy who had only run for a few months, and a few lean master runners training for the next 10k or half marathon. It was one of those days where running just came easy. The ever-increasing pace kept feeling good. The group had dwindled to four of us at the head of the pack, striding along in step, regular, powerful breathing feeding our muscles' every move, and knowing this is why we run: purely for the joy of the experience. It is why we buy shoes, why we roll out of bed, why we have no problem taking off down a strange road in the middle of the woods.

Having said that, I think we, as runners, need more books about the joys and rewards of running. I write these running thoughts, to those of you who have enjoyed running in the past, and to those of you that will enjoy it tomorrow.

THE WARMUP

She was shopping in Boston at 11:00 on a Monday morning. What else would one want to do on a cloudy April morning? As she passed by a local person, they asked if she was in town for the marathon. Now locals do know the ropes, and they informed her that if she had any notion of seeing the finish, she had better get to the finish line immediately. As my wife made her way down the street, the sky slowly began to send rain drops onto the whole Boston area. She stood in the rain for nearly four hours just to see if I would complete what I had come to attempt. Some say we runners are a bit crazy. Well, it takes a crazy wife to support and accept all that we do. For four hours in the rain, for thousands of clean running clothes, and for accepting my countless shoe purchases - I dedicate this effort to my wife. I appreciate her thirty-five years of understanding what I do and I love her for allowing me to do what I love.

PEACHBOWL MARATHON, ATLANTA, GEORGIA, 1971

"A Minnesota Kid Goes to Atlanta"

"Hello Mom, how ya doing?"

"Oh really? That ready for Christmas already? That's great. By the way can I go to Atlanta, Georgia for a few days before Christmas?"

"Why? Oh….well…. I want to run a marathon with some friends."

"Ah… no, I won't be getting paid for it. I just want to run 26 miles…. yes, I think I can run that far….Five of us are going to go together in a buddy's station wagon….Well no, we are going to camp out so I should be able to afford it..."

"Well, yes, I agree it is a bit crazy and doesn't totally make sense, but we would like to do it anyway….Oh yah, some of them have run that far before, they know what they are doing…."

"Great! See you a few days before Christmas. Yes I have a ride home and the guys will pick me up at the farm. Take care….See you soon….Uh, thanks…. Bye…."

Wow, that went well, I guess. There I was: an 18 year old college freshman and I was going to travel from Minnesota to Georgia with four teammates and attempt to run 26 miles in a city I had never seen. Some of my friends were confident, so I guessed what the heck? I mean, what could go wrong? What would be the worst that could happen? I guess I decided not to think about it that way.

Several things in life had already gone well, so I had no reason to believe this should be any different. However, somewhere along the way I had learned that preparation for an event goes a long ways towards that event being successful.

One afternoon, a little later than I should have gotten started, I headed north. There was about a mile of running in town beyond the college before the highway headed into the country. Up north the traffic is minimal, things besides the wind do howl, and crazy people have been known to do crazy things. I didn't take any water, I didn't tell anyone where I was going, and I did go alone. The whim, the desire, the need, for the first time in my life, was to run 20 miles. I needed to know that I could do that. I needed to privately convince myself that I could do that.

The furthest I had ventured out to this point in my life was 16 miles, and I had discovered an ability that I could handle running for a long period of time. The one thing I hadn't considered was German Shepherd dogs. Three of them interrupted me on the out portion of the run. It was still light out, I had seen all of them before they came close to me, and none had tasted my flesh, so far. When I gladly reached the small green sign that indicated the small town of twenty-six people that was ten miles away, I was feeling fine. I knew I had been working, but things felt normal. My biggest concern was really the dog problem, but sometimes you just have to believe things are going to work out. All three of them greeted me in their not-so-friendly fashion and one more, blacker than the others, scared the goose bumps onto my skin. I out-yelled, out-sprinted, and out-stared all of them, making it past their personal portions of the highway. As can be common on a long run, when I hit about mile fourteen, I just went into oblivion. Dusk was becoming reality, the temperature was dropping down into the lower 30s, and the steps just kept on coming. Stride after stride, occasional bright car lights of workers going home for supper, feet barely visible as the toes hit the pavement of the next step, steady breathing on a quiet winter night, I covered the miles. I was still running strong as I felt myself coming into town. At about mile nineteen I passed an illuminated cross on a church. I stopped, for the first time in nineteen miles, with one prevailing thought entering my mind, "Shall I not pause in the light to remember God?" I did that, and confidently jogged back to the college dorm.

December, 1971- The first two guys showed up at my parents' home and we headed to St. Paul to meet the other two. The down-sized brown station wagon would be "home" for the next couple of days. The first part of the drive was easy as we were all psyched about the Christmas holiday, what had been, and now what was to come. We left White Bear Lake, Minnesota, on a late afternoon, and sometime during that long trek across Wisconsin, it began to be a bit boring. Before long I was sound asleep in the back, probably exhausted from college tests, traveling, and pre-trip excitement.

Later that night, when it was pitch dark, or as dark as it can be in the middle of Chicago, one of the guys was shaking me awake. "Say Barny, it's your turn to drive."

"Huh, uh what, oh, o.k., no problem." I crawled out, walked around to the driver's side of the car and got in. My first question was, "Where the heck are we?" Their response sort of scared me, having never been in a city larger than Minneapolis during my eighteen years of living.

"Oh, we are somewhere near downtown Chicago and we are lost." They were casual, and I was amazed they were depending on the farm kid from central Minnesota to solve this problem. They were good friends, but I had only known them for four months, so it made the situation interesting. As I was just about fully awake, I glanced over to my left, and between two different highways a frightened deer sprinted uncontrollably to who knows where. I guess you could say both of us were slightly out of our element. Eventually the map started to make sense to my co-pilot and we were once again headed southeast, Georgia bound.

We were certainly a strange hodge-podge. Our vagabond bunch was made up of a senior with several marathons behind him, two rookie juniors, a sophomore who was also entering his first marathon, and me. It was obviously my first, but that didn't seem to matter. We were traveling, we were on our way, and I was excited about the possibilities. I had finished my first season of college cross country and had logged hundreds of miles with the group, so the confidence wasn't totally ridiculous. I had also done that solo 20 mile run that had gone well. Still somehow, driving on the interstate at 4:30 in the morning the rational side of my thinking was in strong debate with why I was really here.

The rest of the drive to Atlanta went well with only one more late night experience seeming to have an effect on our group dynamics. The following evening as three of us were sleeping in the car, the driver, Kurt, who had the least amount of common sense, abruptly slammed on the breaks and brought the car immediately down from 60 to 25 miles an hour. We were all instantly awake, worried, and wondering what had happened. Kurt responded, "What do you mean, the big orange construction sign said 'Speed limit 25 miles per hour; Men Working!' We tried to convince Kurt that it was probably not a big thing in the middle of the night! A couple of the guys never let him forget that move.

Being five guys from Minnesota, we were ecstatic to arrive in Atlanta at 48 degrees. Being acclimated to northern Minnesota, we didn't wear much for jackets which amazed several people, all who were wearing the heaviest winter coats they owned. The most amazed were the campground people and those that lived near there. Only two other groups were camping and we were the only ones sleeping in a tent. Actually, we thought nothing of it. Just more crazy experiences by some young guys ready to challenge a 26 mile run. Somehow sleeping out in our nice cozy sleeping bags at 40 degrees seemed like nothing compared to the upcoming run.

Doing the typical tourist thing, we were able to check out Underground Atlanta. In my memory it seems as though it was mysterious, dark, and primarily made up of bars and nightclubs. My prevailing memory is that we were not supposed to really be there. I had the opportunity to go back to underground Atlanta in 1996 for the Olympic Track Trials and it is primarily underground shopping and eating now, and quite family orientated. We also did some shopping in the city prior to running the marathon. We all went to a running store and bought "Tiger" racing flats. They were amazingly light, had an extreme lack of cushioning, and of course, totally new. That's another part of being an 18 year-old rookie: some things may work out, but some things are just plain dumb.

Finally race day arrived. Forty trophies were available for the Peach Bowl Marathon. Today's well known runner and author Jeff Galloway was involved, and there were over 150 runners that started the race. The course was very residential, lots of southern homes, lots of turns, and many different roads were used. I started out in a very conservative mode, last for our group, and was just smart enough to be very patient. About 12 miles into it, I remember my feet starting to hurt. We had spent the evening before the race in a motel, and we had a room for the night after. All of us had proudly worn our shoes in the motel room the night before. Mine were pure white, about 1/4 inch of sole, and much less cushioning than my feet were used to. About at this point in the race I finally questioned the wisdom of wearing a new shoe to run 26 miles for the first time in my life. My confidence level was still high even if my intelligence level was certainly in question.

While not being the most gifted athlete in the world, my natural endurance has always served me well. At the half-way point of my first marathon, that endurance started to surface as a quiet encouragement to keep pushing the pace. I slowly started to pass a few other individuals, some who where slowing from too hard of an early pace, but some that simply were on a pace that I was able to exceed. A few miles further down the course I spotted my first teammate that I had been in contact with since the starting line. Kurt was moving okay, a little off his normal gait, and his pace had obviously slowed a bit. There is always that point where you wonder how to deal with a friend who is not running as well as you are feeling, and what to say to encourage them on their quest. As I caught Kurt, we ran together for a couple hundred meters; then, I wished him well and went back to my forward assault on the field.

The course almost assaulted me at one time during the race. The marathon was run completely in the metro area, it included lots of turns and road changes. At one point, I came to an intersection that was controlled by a stop sign. Some not-so-friendly citizen came cruising through, evidently planning on sneaking through the runners, and either didn't see me or didn't care and just missed taking my legs out from under me. This was not the most pleasant problem to encounter after having covered sixteen miles. I did hit his car hood with both of my hands to avoid going down and bounced back just fine, but it triggered my brain to stay alert and be aware of what was happening.

At mile 16, I tried to distract myself from the pain in my feet. I knew if I could deal with it and continue striding, things would work out fine. A small amount of red on my left shoe, however, was cause for concern. This was my first marathon, but not my first blood blister from running. Psychological ploys and bargains with self began to jump at me from all sides. Nearing the 23 mile mark everything changed when I spotted my next buddy from college. I had still been continually sighting, catching, and gradually going by some of the field and working my way up. Now I had a new person to try and close the gap with, someone I knew, an experienced upper classman who had more racing experience. Passing mile 24, I was within 80 or 90 meters of him, and slowly progressing forward. Some time during that mile there was a look I will never forget. As he approached the top of a hill, Larry turned gradually to the left and saw me. Our eyes met in recognition and understanding. He wore the look of respect and knowledge. I didn't gain anymore on him and we finished with about the same gap as the marathon ended. My first run of 26 miles, 385 yards, ended on the middle of the straightaway of a cinder track at Westminster College.

How does the body react after running for 2 hours, 54 minutes? The nerves want to keep firing, the muscles want to keep their movement patterns, and the feet, well, they want to fall off. At least they did in my first marathon in a new pair of non-cushioned shoes. Finding the teammates and seeing that all four of us had indeed survived, we started to look for our fifth and final runner, Kurt. He came in before too long, looking uncomfortable, and sweating a lot (as he always seemed to do). He did his partial lap on the track, came to that same finish line, and just kept running! "Kurt, you're done, stop, Kurt stooooopppp!" He could not stop running. Two of us somehow ran across the infield, as best we could, grabbed him and had to do some deliberate reality therapy. One of us slapped him, we both held on to him, and finally convinced him it was over! We had all finished the Atlanta Peach Bowl Marathon. I had found my first 26 mile, 385 yard finish line.

The awards presentation took place in a gym somewhere in Atlanta. I clearly remember struggling to sit in the wooden bleachers with a body that was not very comfortable. Jeff Galloway, who of course has done many great things for runners over the years, and a friend of his, were the presenters. He himself had finished 5th in 2 hours and 28 minutes and now he was up handing out the awards. The boys from Minnesota had caught their attention and we were awarded 4 of the 40 trophies handed out that day. I had finished 33rd in a time of 2:54:49. Honestly all my memories except those poor aching feet are positive, so it must have been a good experience. I do recall some references to raw hamburger as we examined and tried to repair our tender feet that evening in the motel room. Mine were bad, dear old Kurt just always had blister problems so it was normal for him. My other buddy, Andy... well, let's just say he had one of the best performances with a quality 10nth place finish in 2 hours and 33 minutes, but he was #1 for the ugliest feet in Atlanta, Georgia, that evening. Post-race healing would be slow and he could barely walk that night and the next day. What is that old adage, "No Pain, No Gain." For us it may have been more accurate to say, "New shoes don't do well on a 26 mile run!"

Lesson learned: New challenging things can be scary and fill us with doubts, but they can also be a truly positive experience.

A FARM BOY BEGINS TO RUN

It was 1965, and it was not uncommon for coaches to smoke cigarettes. No one really questioned that; I didn't dislike it or complain much, although I do recall a few indirect, sarcastic comments once I knew my coaches well enough to get personal. The golf course was only a mile from the junior high, and being that it was 1965, it was also acceptable for our group to jog there on our own every day. We would leave school, and we must have been instructed to take it easy, because we always did. We would run down the side streets laughing, joking, jogging, and sharing the stories of the day. Even though it was a mile over and a mile back it was easy for most or us, and my memories of those jogs to practice are very positive. We knew we would work hard when we got there, but hard work was fine with most of us.

Intervals, team members, slower runners disappearing, we somehow became a team. A very diverse group: a dentist's son, a poor farmer's son, a prosperous farmer's son, a shaky farmer's son, and me. We were all holding our own in the classroom, even though I don't think any of us worked very hard at it. Hard work was really reserved for practice. None of us were afraid to race. Since junior high our coaches had us learning not to be afraid to do our best and to know that in itself would be good enough. Somehow we moved from a middle of the pack crew to a very competitive group that other teams really had to worry about. Maybe it was happening because of those summer intervals I had done across the hayfield. Some of those were actually done in a pair of Dad's tight-fitting bedroom slippers, a foot covering very similar to the racing shoes I would eventually wear in my first marathon. It's too bad I didn't have the insight to market those first racing flats. Maybe part of our team's success was happening because of those eight mile runs I did from our farm into town on summer mornings before I worked all day at the local creamery. Maybe our team was just a bunch of skinny guys who started to believe they were good runners. But somehow we had become a team. Coach Joe had a couple of favorite things he seemed to like to have his team do. They were interesting workouts, some which would make a psychologist or a behavior management expert really wonder, but they worked for us. One of his training methods was the run as far as you can down a gravel road in 45 minutes, and then turn back and return to school. (I wonder if coach ever knew that a few of the guys climbed a tree one day and sat in it for half an hour or more.) Our main group simply cruised and tried to get further out on the road each time we ran that workout. For some reason most of us also worked extra hard to make it back faster than we went out. Another practice was to play soccer on a fairway of our local golf course. The course was about 200 yards long with the goals at either end, which was supersized, to say the least. Maybe we were dumb, maybe we knew better, but we loved it. I imagine it was an easy coaching day for Coach Joe and most of the time it was a great workout for us, if we survived without an injury. Another favorite training method seemed to be Friday morning time trials on the golf course. Unless the meet schedule didn't allow it, we raced each other every Friday morning. Now in Minnesota, in late October, racing barefoot on a course with several oak trees can be interesting. Serious nimble stepping around acorns and twigs, and sometimes early morning frost had to be a questionable training practice. However, many of these techniques did motivate us to continue getting better and faster at this running thing. They caused me to believe I was capable of confronting any obstacle in my way to be the best runner I could be. Maybe it was that 60's era of history, maybe we were just insane, but we did what we were told to do, and we did it as well as we were able. There really was not a great runner in the bunch. But as a team we were toned and strong, and evidently ready for that championship season.

Conference championships my senior year were upon us. It was going to be an exciting day as we headed to the small town thirteen miles to the east of us. Typical meet preparation was under way and we were assembling at the starting line. That line gets a little long when eight to ten teams get ready to race, but there we were, and it was time, and another race was about to start. We were stripped down to our racing clothes, spikes on, poised and ready. I had my usual left foot forward, ready to spring into action. But somehow the starter was unclear in his commands, and half the field on the left started to go, then stepped back, and our side took off and we were gone. Either they couldn't or they didn't bother, but the race was not called back. There we were, a team to be reckoned with anyway, and we had just gotten our best start ever off the line.

With what was really a false start, I felt unsure if I should actually keep running or not, but by now everyone was on the course and on their way. I looked around and the race was on and my entire team was in the top 20 or so and running west and going about our business. It was our second to the last race we would ever run as a team, and race we did. I believe we took first place honors that day, because I know we were the top-rated conference team going into the region meet the following week.

Regional championships were held in the Minneapolis area. We would be racing the metro boys, who really only lived an hour to the south, but it was like going into someone else's territory. Small-town thinking can be a terrible thing when you are supposed to race and do your best. Coach Joe knew all that, and being the analytical math teacher that he was, he quickly showed us with numbers and his quiet confidence in us that we would be able to go down there and run with the best. We had worked with him for six years, we had rolled out of bed for him at 6:15 on Friday mornings, and we believed in what he had to say.

Weather can be a gamble in Minnesota in late October, but it was a day where the weather would not be a contributing factor. Cool, but very do-able, and we could run our best on such a day on a flat golf course in Minneapolis. We all mixed it up well, held our own, all running in the top half of the competition, and our races felt good. I was fourth for the team, my usual position. We had missed qualifying for state by two spots, finishing as the fourth team in one of the toughest regions in our state, and had enjoyed doing our best as a team.

The family farm, prosperous and huge was still there. The guys, who I had come to know so well, were still there. November would arrive in a couple of days and there was spring track just a few months in the future. But this year's unique cross-country team's experience had just come to an end. I had survived winning, losing, injury, success, happiness, friendship and togetherness all through running. We had all done that together. For me, it was so important, and felt so right, that it was destined to be a part of the rest of my life.

FARM SCENE - The hay field in front is where I did my sprint training in Dad's bedroom slippers.

Lesson learned: A team, or running with others, brings out the best in all of us.

THE TRACK

High school track and field was a competitive sport in my hometown. Past teams had created some good tradition, and the 440 yard track was one of the better cinder tracks in the area. My sophomore year resulted in my first "letter" as a high school athlete. It also provided one of the most clarifying and memorable moments of my life as a runner.

It was the home-town invitational, and the races were run in the late afternoon and early evening. It was a typical cool, spring evening with fresh, crisp air accompanying dusk. As I warmed up and stretched with the other underclassmen, the football lights came on. It wasn't really that dark yet, but it helped set the tone for the mile run that was the next running event on the track. There were about five teams competing, and we had several entrants, two of which were my senior brother and his buddy who were favored to place that evening. About twelve of us toed the line and were anxiously awaiting the starter's instructions that would send us around the oval.

The race was underway, and I tucked into the inside rail in about ninth place, just starting to feel the pace of the race and the evening. I spent the first two laps in that position, and just kept my eye on things up ahead. At the beginning of lap three, realizing I was over half way through the race and I still felt good, I moved up one spot into 8th place just before we ran the first curve. On the back straightaway another guy was running a pace that slowed my long strides down a bit, and I moved into seventh place still feeling strong. Looking ahead there was one more out of town runner, and then my brother's buddy with my brother ahead of him. I came off the last curve of lap three and powered by the guy in sixth, coming into scoring position and right on the heels of our two senior runners. Feeling it was my day, I started lap four by passing both seniors, holding my position for the entire lap and finishing in fourth place. I suppose you would say I had arrived. It was great to be the top miler that day for our high school and I began to discover what I was able to do. There was no sibling rivalry that day, and both seniors were honestly happy for me, each knowing he wasn't that strong a runner. Besides, my brother's main event was the high jump and he was the individual winner of that event during the same meet

Many years later I would come back and win a small, local race that ended on that same track. It is now a beautiful all-weather facility at the exact same location. That victory some thirty years later was a proud and happy event, but not as significant as that fourth-place finish had been in high school.

Confidence is a special thing. That sophomore race in high school inspired me to continue to discover who I was as a runner and as a person. It also, unfortunately, labeled me as the school miler and virtually forced me to run that distance the rest of my high school career. Luckily, that factor didn't ruin my joy of running and what running could do for me. This early confidence helped me continue discovering all the possible successes within the sport of running. I know that such possibilities are attainable for so many others as well if they are willing to get out there. It just worked out that another classmate of mine and a guy one year younger became premiere two milers and I was always the one to race the mile. In spite of that we were still a team.

It was the sixties and early seventies and many of us in high school ran both winter and summer, in addition to competing in fall cross country and spring track. Our coaches were dedicated and a little crazy. I will never forget the "Pain Pit" workout. It consisted of running 220 yards thirty times, and then running four more 220's under thirty-five seconds before completing the daily workout. If at anytime a runner felt he could not handle it, he was simply invited to sit on the pole vault pits, in other words, the "pain pit" and was allowed to sit there the rest of the workout. Somehow it was not done in a way that ridiculed or demeaned. Instead, I remember a lot of encouragement. This was a team workout, including throwers, jumpers, sprinters and everyone. As the whole team circled the track time after time a true sense of team pride and accomplishment were instilled. Fortunately, I never entered the pain pit, and I thrived on these kinds of workouts. Perhaps this had something to do with my special treatment during the winter months. Somehow all winter long I was excused, during the middle of the school day, to run a four-mile loop. Yes, the school knew about it, and coach even provided me with an extra wind-proof sweat suit to protect me on the coldest days. I was ready for the "Pain Pit" kind of workouts once the season began.

By senior year, our rigorous training and team pride had produced a well rounded, talented, and competitive group of track athletes. We worked hard, we worked together, and we had lots of success. We were not angels, and some may not have always done one-hundred percent of the work, but somehow our coaches inspired us to believe in and support each other.

As we did in cross country, we headed to the Twin Cities for tournaments in the spring of our senior year. Spring track tournaments often conflicted with graduation, as a result we needed to rush back for graduation that evening. As we finished our last bus ride together and arrived at the high school, we did one of those crazy fast, hurried showers and I headed into the gym and slid into my First Chair Trombone spot. The band was getting ready to play our featured song for that evening that I had been allowed to select, and I was completely thrilled. That day for the first time in 42 years our Track Team had won the Regions 4AA Track and Field Championship. Six of my team mates, one of them being our top sprinter and my best friend, were going on to the state tournament. Even though I had only scored one simple point, of course in the mile run, I had run my best time of 4 minutes and 41 seconds. That was the fastest I had ever and could ever run up to that point, and our high school band proudly began the song, "Let There Be Peace on Earth." It really inspired me to perform that song after experiencing a very good day on the track and in life.

To this day whenever I drive by the Coon Rapids High School track on Highway 10 in north Minneapolis, I still reflect on that final high school race. It must have been significant, it must have been positive, because it made me crave running more races in my future. We spent the night after graduation at Coach's house, eating sloppy joes and being together. Our team's last meet was over and the victory was a great reason to have a party.

Lesson learned: As life goes by, certain events occur that are really awesome. We need to celebrate the good times!

04

RUNNING THROUGH COLLEGE

It was an early spring evening, and I was spending too much time on the phone. The college coach from the metro area continued to talk highly of his program. The information he was sharing did sound exciting and challenging, but his institution had made the mistake of upsetting our household. The early seventies saw quite a drastic change in the way college funding was being allotted, and my "scholarship" which I had earned had been cut in half. The telephone was a wall mount model, hanging at about five feet and located above our grey wooden, kitchen chair. My mom came in the kitchen after awhile and was finally able to get my attention. The coach had started to ramble, and he was looking for a commitment on my part. When my eyes met mom's, she mouthed the words that I should just tell him no. Even though we had talked about this before, I struggled with the idea of refusing a scholarship to a coach and a college that I certainly had an interest in. That night, however, I refused my scholarship.

One private school also had an interest in my running talent. The coach had watched a few of my races and was a very nice man. However, St. Olaf College in Northfield, Minnesota was one of the most expensive in the state, and I just could not see the value, for me personally, in going there. (Many years later our daughter would attend St. Olaf and have a great experience being an "Ole" and singing "Um-Yah-Yah".)

My next visit was to Bemidji State College in northern Minnesota during the first part of May. It was one of those unbelievably perfect spring days with the temperature in the seventies and the sun shining brightly in the awesome, bright blue sky. I checked out the campus, met the coach, and went wading in the waters of Lake Bemidji. This is not a commercial for northern Minnesota or Bemidji State, but I just had that feeling that this is where I wanted to be. I had a cousin and his wife and a former neighbor from back home who were upperclassmen here and were on schedule to graduate. All of these factors seemed to give Bemidji State a positive rating. Because things had fallen apart for me in the Twin Cities, Bemidji State may have been my choice by default, and I signed up for classes the following fall. Meeting the coach was pleasant, but not exactly exciting. He was a big guy, a former national "javelin" champion from Illinois, and he did not have $1 to give me for a scholarship. That didn't really bother me, since I was a complete walk-on and not really a fantastic high school athlete, but it did not impress me either.

I returned home to complete that awesome experience of senior year of high school track, to graduate, and get ready for trying to make my first college team. Our farm was eight miles out in the country, and my summer job was at the local creamery in town. This was my second summer of dumping milk cans and helping make and package butter. I knew every inch of what that place had to offer. Being the only young person there I was also called upon to do every errand there was to do. I also knew that in the back of the feed store bathroom there was a shower. Ah yes, an opportunity. I began, with quite a bit of regularity, to run the eight miles to work in the morning, then shower, work all day, and usually run part way home in the evening. My oldest brother had a construction job that summer, and he would either pick me up at work or find me along the way and give me a ride the rest of the way home. Additional preparation for my new running team consisted of a few evening runs, farm chores, and a few occasional sprints across the hayfields at night.

I had honestly never been to northern Minnesota prior to that spring visit. Moving there was going to be a small shock, but I was ready to be independent, and eager to try new things. Being cast into an entirely new situation with no other high school classmates attending Bemidji State, could have been frightening to some people. Personally, I thrived on it, and the biggest reason was joining the cross country team. The bonds made with high school teammates didn't come close to the camaraderie of my college cross county teammates, sharing literally everything there is to share in life. Along with the college courses, we learned many different things in many different ways. It was a complete education. My most important lessons learned during college came from my coach, teammates, and competition.

That big guy who we called "coach" had a reputation of being a hard-nose. Actually, I saw very little of that side of him. My first introduction to Coach Robert J. Eudeikis was when he issued me a pair of Adidas running shoes. This is nothing against that shoe company, because in later years I have purchased several pairs of Adidas running shoes. But in 1971, the selection was very limited. I had purchased a pair of the original leather Tiger running shoes in high school for $10.50. They were white with a corrugated type sole, and blue and red markings on the sides. I dutifully wore the newly issued

Adidas with the college jock, shirt, and green and white socks the first day of practice. It was great to meet the guys and we had a nice easy six mile run, but my feet hurt. I stuck around after practice and told coach he could keep his shoes, and I would wear my own until he could get me a better pair. The next day we did five timed miles, I performed well enough that I would be running varsity for the first meet the following week. At that meet I made the top six for the squad and by the next practice Coach Eudeikis issued me a new pair of Tigers. My running career moved to the next level.

(My recent purchase of retro Nikes is a reoccurrence of the third pair of

running shoes I ever owned. The Tigers mentioned were similar but with red and blue stripes. This Nike Leather Cortez style was state of the art in 1972. I saw them in a store in 2007 and I just had to buy them! They are white with red swoosh and trim.)

"Coach" would prove to be one of the nicest, helpful, and most realistic people I had ever met. He was available, loved to visit, and expected us to stop by his office on a regular basis. It wasn't something he scheduled, or was formal about, but just something we seemed to want to do. He knew a lot about what it takes to be a good runner. He understood distance running, this is not a simple thing to understand. When you run for 16, 25, or 32 minutes in a race a lot goes on in your mind and your body. When you train at 50, 70, or 90 miles a week, a lot goes on in your mind and your body. He was great about helping us deal with the highs and the lows, and he helped motivate us to work hard at becoming our best. He chose to write up weekly workouts on the team bulletin board so we always knew what was expected of us and most of us were very willing to do that and more. Sometimes, I was a little too determined to do every task of every workout he designed. Once, while injured, I was limping around the track trying to complete the planned workout. He called me over and said he didn't want to see me at practice for a week! I was angry for a little while, but it was exactly what I needed to hear and what I needed to do to get back to healthy running.

Remember those four other guys from the team mentioned in Mile 1 and the Atlanta trip? They were what it was really all about, and of course there were many more teammates too. We had already grown that close from September to December in my freshman year, but after four years together we were closer than many brothers. We trained, planned, practiced and raced together. The mutual support and belief in what we, and our teammates, could accomplish was very positive. During one particular workout early in my career, three of the guys were up ahead on the road, with me following them from about fifteen meters behind. We were still three miles from getting back to school, just striding along on a cool fall day. All at once they stopped right in the middle of the run. I caught up to them and asked what was wrong. They responded, "You have been back there following us for the past twenty minutes. Now get up here and run with us." They wisely pointed out to me that I could maintain their pace so there was no reason in the world why I shouldn't be up running directly with them. It really became a survival technique to maintain a quality pace and work hard with others pushing right along with you. It made me realize I could train at their level and I became so much more confident that I could perform at the collegiate level.

Much of those four years is a long, pleasant blur of activity. Upperclassmen graduated and new freshmen came along every year. Through it all we had that bond and comradeship that makes a team a special unit of young men. Some of those teammates I now often coach against because a half dozen or so are active coaches across out state. Some teammates I have lost track of, but that doesn't mean I don't recall with fond memories what they once meant to me and to our college. My closest friend, a 400 runner who joined cross country just to be with the guys, actually ran his final race and passed away from cancer at the age of forty-nine. He was always healthy and never overweight, but just unexpectedly found he had cancer of the liver and passed away four months later. He was a great guy, and we were best men in each other's weddings. He had uncertainties of how to pass from his life here on earth to eternal life in heaven, but never had any doubt that was where he was headed. One of the last times I visited him in the hospital he was trying to be comfortable in the recliner and simply asked me to lie in his hospital bed next to the recliner and hold his hand. I had "held his hand" through cross country workouts and other experiences of life. We had trained together, worked together, and experienced many young adult moments together in life. Lyle was always a bit naive about some of life's happening, so often I would teach him and watch him experience some of life's lessons. He also taught me about death and about facing the ultimate adversity any of us will ever encounter. Delivering the eulogy at his funeral, I was able to express the happiness, peace, and acceptance Lyle discovered throughout his life's journey. I actually had a great experience presenting the eulogy at his funeral, because he had made it so very clear that I should do that for him. It was not all sorrow and pain, because that is not what life, and even the end of his life, was all about. There is happiness, there is peace, in all situations, if only we can work in our own minds at discovering and accepting that happiness and peace.

Another college friend had never really been confident enough to join the team. He had some success in high school in track and field but like so many others lacked the confidence to come out for the team in college. Through classes and intramural basketball I had become friends with Jerry and convinced him one spring to join our ranks and become a part of the college track team. I don't think he ever scored a point in meets, but he loved being a part of the group and held his own just fine in practice. He went on to become a math teacher and a very involved coach and is head track coach at one of the schools in our region. He has coached many regional championship teams and many state competitors in a fine career as a teacher and coach. Jerry is proof that many times the skills learned and confidence gained through team competition extend far beyond the victories and medals earned on the track. During our senior year we both were taking social dance class. Ballroom type dancing used to be a big part of life for many rural Minnesotans as they were growing up. After class one day I told Jerry what a great dancer my partner had been that day and encouraged him to try and dance with her some day for class. They just celebrated their 33rd anniversary, have raised three children, and have had a great life together.

My college cross country career was probably my most memorable. Along with the early shoe issue there was another experience that became very conclusive as to the fact I would be a varsity runner. We had a time trial on our home golf course during my freshmen year and I was determined to qualify for the team. It was a five mile race and I followed the two guys I needed to catch for the first two miles. Starting the next perimeter of the course, I made a strong move going into an uphill portion of the course, leaving the two of them behind. One, a fellow freshman, followed me in from a distance. The other runner, a senior, dropped out of the race when he couldn't stay with me. He claimed he wasn't feeling well, and that is why I had beaten him. Luckily coach honored and respected what I had done, and that senior never did finish ahead of me again. I had the experience of leading the team as our top runner a few times my senior year and I was one of the captains of our team. Again, I had not secured a scholarship before I started my college career, but "Coach" came up with a few dollars my last two years and helped me, through people he knew, to get jobs starting track meets and supervising community sporting venues so I did fine making ends meet. I was fortunate to be able to improve anywhere from 20 to 30 seconds on my best time during each of the years that I competed. As my best times kept improving I began to race at very close to five minutes per mile pace and became a strong upper echelon runner. My final race was my best one, and I was able to go to the national qualifying meet and miss nationals by only four places. The top fifteen qualified for nationals and I was nineteenth. I was thrilled to be that close and had averaged 4:57 per mile in the last race of my college career. Realistically, I would have been one of the slowest runners in the national cross country race and, although it would have been a great trip, I had a good run and was very pleased with what I was able to accomplish.

Track and field was also a positive experience for me. There too I became captain, but this time by default. Two of my senior classmates were elected captain at the end of our junior year but they were both injured the next January when the season started. Along with another teammate, the two of us became captains for our final competitive season. My first college victory was a bit of a scam. We went to the southern part of the state for an outdoor meet and although there were five colleges there it was a low key affair, especially in the distance events. I was racing 5000 meters and doing fine with two laps to go, running in third place. My two buddies that were in first and second were not very far ahead, but all at once I felt the pace slow, and they came back to me. They had discussed it and decided it was my turn to win a college race. They continued to back off a bit and told me to take it home for the win. Like I said, college teammates are very special, and it felt good to be the first to cross the finish line. At the same time, it felt even better to realize what they had done for me.

Two months before that 5000 victory I was racing at the University of Minnesota indoor facility in the Northwest Open track meet and had a significant break through in my track running. I had raced there in high school and my freshmen year of college, and the facility was not what it is today. It was a dirt facility, with reddish brown sand like surface. Long time coach Roy Griak was a younger man in those days, and his smile and enthusiasm have long been special to many of us who are part of the running and track programs in Minnesota. Today, Mr. Griak has one of the better cross country meets in the nation named after him and many collegiate and high school runners race on the University of Minnesota Golf Course every fall. Roy himself used to line up the heats for our races. He would call up certain people by times and shake the old pill bottle and pull out numbers for our lane assignments. So there I was, probably the fifth or sixth time I had faced him, knowing he was very enthusiastic about what he was doing, and getting placed in my lane for the two mile run. My sweats were full of the dust from warming up, the air had its own unique smell, the haze from the dust hung in the air, as we got the lane assignments for our race. Mr. Griak was hyper as usual, very directive, but helping us get the job done. I proceeded to get my placement and headed over to the starting area. Things were feeling right.

Our team had made our trip down the night before, traveling in four station wagons, and we had stayed in the motel and were planning to eat at one of coaches famous all you can eat places after the meet was over. The starter called us to the line, I was just excited for the day, and the gun went off. Even though the track was eight laps to the mile, I have always been a calculating individual and to this day had never dipped below ten minutes for a two mile race. I came through the mile in 4:50 and had the overwhelming thought that all I had to do was run a five minute mile and I would finally pass that barrier. Being my second year of college, I now had a finishing kick, which never used to exist, and it had started to get stronger. I had a powerful race that day and was able to pass four more people during the last half-mile and ran a two mile race in 9:56, for my first sub ten minute race. It was one of those special days and somehow it felt extra good to be able to do it at the University of Minnesota.

The spring of my junior year I did decide that if I was going to continue to improve and do well I needed more improvement on my kick. Usually about two days a week I spent time after the regular team practice staying on the track and doing a series of 200's. Most of the time I would run ten to fifteen of them, and about the second time I was doing them a spring football player that I knew stopped by and asked what I was up to. He was in the process of trying to improve his overall conditioning. As a result we ended up having several spring sessions together doing the same extra workout, but for different reasons. Ironically, when it came time for my first Boston qualifier a few years later, he would show up on the starting line of the twenty-six mile race. From a physical standpoint it was really strange to see a former 260 pound lineman at a marathon, but knowing how his mind worked, I was not all that surprised.

Another very pleasant experience happened during my senior year at the St. John's Invitational. St. John's is a school more widely known for their success in football, but they also host some small college and high school track meets. We were at a small meet with about six or seven teams and I no longer even remember which place I finished. I do know I placed, however, and I was able to continue my time improvements by running a three mile in 14 minutes and 52 seconds. This was the new indoor record for our school, and it would be broken in years to come, but it was another milestone for me to reach as I got my name in the record books.

As in cross country, nationals qualifying did escape me. However, once again I would give it a good shot, and I did get close. By the time my senior year rolled around, the team generally needed my efforts in both the three mile and the six mile runs at most of our meets. That is 36 laps of racing, sometimes taking place in one day. For that reason, most of my training took place off the track. However, I was able to place in many of our meets and lead our team most of the time in both races. I ended up getting within 40 seconds of qualifying for nationals with a 31:20 six mile time. I completely felt I had given it my best and was very proud of what I had been able to accomplish.

* * * * *

The following is part of the eulogy I did for my former college teammate. One of the final things he asked me to do as he was dying in the hospital was to lay on the hospital bed while he sat in the recliner. We just sat and talked because it was what he needed at the time He was very certain of how his life had been, he was very certain of where his future was headed, he just was uncertain of how we get from one stage to the other. He put his hand in mine, and we had a great visit..

Hold My Hand Lord

"Why don't you just hold my hand?
Crawl up here, next to me,
Get comfortable now-
And just hold my hand."
The hospital, gown, hospital bed,
shots, liquid food, people checking, poking,
....just hold my hand.
Wherever my now small steps take me-
....down the tile hall with my IV tree,
....to my couch in my cozy living room,
....to the elevator and actually leaving this place,
....around my house to my beautiful back yard,
....down the aisle of my church to sit in that pew,
just hold my hand Lord.
How long has it been here?
They don't seem to know.
I mostly lie here and wonder
how did it, in MY body, start to grow.
Too much uncertainty, too many tests
If you keep me peaceful, I'll be able to rest.
Fear, concern, for others and me,
Anger, helplessness, and even apathy.
Which chemo to use, or maybe radiation?
Passing the time, but sick of television.
Lord, it's comforting having you here all the time,
"Just crawl up here, get comfortable,
and put your hand in mine."

Lesson learned: You really have to know yourself well in the last lap of your race and of your life.

LONGEST DAY MARATHON, BROOKINGS, SOUTH DAKOTA, 1975

"Life is not a sprint, it is a marathon."

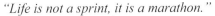

    The one person I spent most of my time with at college was Mr. Carrier. We lived together for four years. He was always happy, always crazy, and one of the most talented people I have ever known. We were co-captains of cross country our senior year, and we virtually ran the lettermen's club for the college since he was president and I was vice president. We made and subsequently ate more popcorn than anyone probably ever did because we worked at almost every home athletic event those last two years of college, becoming concession stand professionals.

    WC came at the running life from the exact opposite direction that I did.

In seventh grade I had tried to be a sprinter, learned early that was not to be my calling, and always approached running after that from the true distance point of view. My roommate came at things from the exact opposite direction. While I approached everything from the quantity perspective, which meant high mileage, he looked at running from the quality point of view, which meant high speed. This probably had something to do with the fact that 1000 meters and 800 meters were his best events. As a matter of fact, thirty years later he still holds one of the 1000 meter records at the college. We would run together a couple of times a week, usually compromising between our two styles or just helping the other guy do whatever kind of workout he needed to get done at the time.

We had a wild idea during November of our senior year to do another marathon. We discovered the "Longest Day Marathon" in Brookings, South Dakota, and decided to give it a shot. The race was a week or two after our final cross country race, and we thought the timing would be great to try another 26 miler. So we left town as early as we could on a Friday, drove my car for eight hours to arrive at our motel and get prepared to run the next day. It wasn't a big field and the weather was in the high 40's, a temperature which through the years I have found to be about the optimum for me to perform well. The course was rather flat and a basic, a huge square with six to seven miles on each side. Does this sound like Dakota? I think it was that race that gave me one of the psychological edges I have often come to use in my racing: Rather than worry how far I have to go or what mile I am on, I simply concentrate on getting to the next turn in good form, feeling good, and maintaining a good pace for my current level of training. Once I complete that stretch and attack that corner, I immediately begin to imagine the same thing for the next turn further along the course. This course had virtually four big turns, spread out quite a bit, with some quick adjusting for the start and finish. The field was small, 150 runners or so, and my task for the day was to cover the 26 miles.

The race at one time had been held on or around June 21st, being the longest day of daylight in this part of the country. Probably due to overheated runners some years, they had kept the name but moved the race to November. The course was interesting and finished on the track at the local university. I sincerely hoped it would not feel like the longest day of running while I attempted to do the marathon.

Off the starting line I immediately sensed the field was not overly talented. We took off on the city streets and with a conservative start I found myself in seventh place and felt totally within myself, knowing that I belonged up that far. My roommate was there to try to cover the distance, and he took a very relaxed approach to the start of the race. As we headed out to the north on the first long stretch, I found it to be a good day to hit and feel my running rhythm. I was moving along nicely and the miles started to clip by. I chose just to stay loose, listen to my body, and just sort of go with the flow. The miles were adding up well with a 6:30 pace feeling comfortable and I approached the first major turn to the right, completing the first eight miles of the run. The next portion, the northern most part of the course, ran from west to east. It was also flat with a nice tar road and a good shoulder. I just kept things going as I had for the first long straight stretch and I was gradually able to overcome first one runner and then another, bringing me to the half-way point in fifth place. By concentrating on just making that next turn without leaving my comfort zone, I was able to continue on pace. With the next right turn we were now headed back to the south and back into town. The previous road had a couple of slight dips and knolls, but this stretch was completely flat, made of smooth tar, and another nice, straight road in the country. Psychologically the culmination of my 26 mile plan and the concentration of getting to that last big turn with strength was unveiling itself as a very good plan. Once again I was watching runner number four and gradually coming up to him over the course of a couple of miles. I was able to eventually catch him too, and after passing him I knew I was in a solid fourth place, but third was nowhere in sight. The last three runners I had passed seemed to be very content to do their thing and really didn't respond much at all when I came up on them. No one really put up a fight or tried to pick up on my pace to "race", they just seemed content to let me make my move and they were going to run their own race. Turn number four gradually became clear, and I knew with less than two miles to go, I was going to be successful.

The rest of the marathon was rather uneventful, and I maintained things quite well. I proceeded into town, entered the local college campus, onto the track, circled it once, and finished my second marathon. Four years of college cross country and many training miles had set me up well for this day. My roommate was there waiting, as he had dropped out somewhere in the middle of the run. Since we were not really interested in hanging around knowing we had an eight hour ride back to college, I asked, in what I thought was a polite way, if I could possibly get my award so we could get started on our journey. The race director was not real happy with my request, but after awhile he said, "Fine, just go to the box and get one of the small trophies." As luck would have it there were three nice, large trophies for the top three places and several little three inch trophies for the next group of finishers. Actually, the award was kind of neat: a gold winged-foot mounted on a two inch square dark piece of wood. I do still have it, and although there was absolutely no celebration involved, I was proud of what I had accomplished. Back at Atlanta I had run 2:54:49 and on this November day I was able to run 2:49:37, so I loved the time and also hoped I had created a pattern. Since I had run my seconds from my first marathon time as my minutes this time around, maybe that could continue and I could someday run a 2:37 marathon! Isn't it crazy how our runner's minds think up those things? For several years I honestly thought I should be able to run a 2:37 marathon. Who knows, if things had gone right, maybe I would have.

Marathoning is so very interesting in a variety of different ways. After feeling so unbelievably good in this one, my body felt just terrible afterwards. I literally threw up three times in the shower at Brookings, South Dakota, after the race and slept most of the way home. I do find a very unique kind of pleasure in allowing my mind and body to run 26 miles, but I never know how my body is going to react once the race is completed. I do have a lot of natural endurance, but from one attempt to the other I have experienced various physical and mental reactions after finishing, or trying to finish, 26 miles, 385 yards. Once again I was very pleased I had experienced 26 miles, as it taught me some more things about myself, and I became even more confident and enthused about my final season of college track.

Lesson learned: Use mental strategies and motivations to help you obtain positive results. Pick a turn or a spot on the course to run to with good form, and a strong pace. As soon as you reach that point, immediately pick a new spot further along the course and use the same way of thinking to get there. Imagine yourself passing that next spot or running through the finish and doing it well.

B.A.A. MARATHON, BOSTON, MASSACHUSETTS 1979
BOSTON #1

It was April of 1979, and I was a young teacher in the working world, full of life, excitement, and energy. Being newly married and having just gotten established in a teaching career, I guess you could say things were moving along nicely. I was working with some ambitious young coaches and some even more ambitious, fine, young athletes and I was riding high on a bizarre idea and plan: I was on my way to the Boston Marathon.

The previous fall I got the urge: Why not run the Boston Marathon, the marathon of all marathons. It just would not go away. Checking things out, I was pleasantly surprised to learn it only cost five dollars to enter (no prize money in those days), and there was, of course, the problem of having to qualify. At that time there was just one qualifying standard for all the runners: Three hours! I was optimistic that I could qualify since I had only been out of college four years and had never stopped running or training. I decided to try and qualify in Minneapolis in what was then the City of Lakes Marathon. That race has since become the famous Twin Cities Marathon of today. Back then it was a course shaped like an 8 that circled two lakes in southwest Minneapolis and repeated the same route four times. The day of the race was nice, about 60 degrees, and things went well. I had typical runner's stiffness that day and even stopped to stretch a time or two. My memory is not always that great, especially compared to the phenomenal recall of my wife, but I vividly recall sitting in the grass on the east side of the lake, stretching my groin and back during one of the laps. My confidence level was high, and that is probably the main reason I qualified. I knew what I had to do and I ran in a very calculated fashion and successfully qualified at 2:58. The typical marathon finish thoughts surfaced. I was glad I was healthy, glad the body had held up, and pleased I was able to execute a good race plan. I had been doing some other racing and training and I wasn't ready for an all out effort, just going about the business of qualifying. This probably helped set me up for a more intense effort the next spring.

I continued to train throughout the winter, which can be a challenge in northern Minnesota. You need to buy shoes with the best tread available, but still a decent running shoe that fits properly. I am one of the world's worst ice- runners and have been known to fall on more than one occasion. Back in college we ran on a trail on the bank of a lake, and during a workout, I fell and scraped myself up as we were crossing one of the wooden bridges. The guys checked me out, then took off on their run while I headed back to the athletic trainer for bandages. For several years the college runners referred to that spot as "Barny's bridge." Thanks to Gortex material on the outside and polypropylene on the inside, I can now survive virtually any conditions. I have always known enough to cover my mouth and nose, especially at the start of a workout on a cold day. After some very painful lessons learned, I purchased proper covering for the male sex organs too. Those poly-lined wind briefs sure make the afterlife of a ten-miler at twenty degrees below zero a lot more comfortable. As I recall, there were times in college where those items were not yet available, and sometimes we came in from the cold with some of the worst thawing-out sensations imaginable.

Basically the winter of '79 was spent building the base and the strength to be set for early spring training. Today, I coach my athletes a lot more specifically than I train, because the only races I really train for now are marathons, and I have a system that works for me. It doesn't match some current published methods and research, but it feels fine and brings about results that I am pleased with. This was the training philosophy I had begun to use in 1979. I would decide what weekly mileage to build up to, then I do a gradual build up to that number. I wanted those peak weeks to be three and four weeks before the marathon. For Boston that peak was 100 miles, so I began a gradual increase up to that level. I tend to have a steadily increasing distance with races throughout the area being done as ways to motivate me and keep me excited about my running. The races are also the best way for me to monitor the success of my training. Back in '79 most of my running was with other people. Solo runs were done as fillers and to make sure the miles were at the level I was looking for.

Being D.I.N.K.s at the time (double income, no kids) the trip was set up without too many problems. My school system was hesitant to give me the days off, especially since I was a new teacher. But, with the proper amount of begging, they granted me the leave, and we were set. Flying out of Minneapolis to Boston was great. Being a person who has always loved flying, I thoroughly enjoyed it. The landing in Boston was really special. You come in over the water and land with the runway being right on the shore. We arrived safely and then had to get to work on deciphering the transfer station and the subway system. My wife is not the most courageous person in the world, but we figured out the subway connection, threw our quarters in the slot and proceeded to enjoy our first subway ride. Our destination, according to the map, was the end of the line out in Cambridge. After a few transfers and a strange first view of the city, we came to our final station. Walking up the steps, we started to really experience Boston.

The station steps led us to an interesting intersection where three roads came together and several small shops were quite close. We entered a small coffee shop that served various teas to my wife's liking, and a huge variety of scrumptious, gourmet muffins with flavors like chocolate almond fudge and blueberry delight. We fell in love with the place and would return often during our stay. Eating their food couldn't have been all bad either. Considering the size of those muffins, they had to be high in carbohydrates.

Leaving the coffee shop we headed north to the Holiday Inn. It was about a seven block walk, past the campus of Harvard University. Being a couple of sentimental "Love Story" fans and knowing the prestige of such an institution, we were in awe as we continued down the street, arms straining to transport our luggage. After a couple of sit-down breaks, we made it to the motel. Thankfully, our reservations were successful, and we moved into our home away from home.

The next three days were fantastic. We walked, and walked, and walked around all the tourist things and explored the colonial landmarks and sites. One day it rained steadily, but we still had a great time. We were darting around town, dodging the raindrops, staying at sites longer than we planned to. I remember a quaint, nostalgic, old fashioned store stacked to the ceiling, and full of everything. We looked for quite awhile and purchased, of course, an umbrella. The Freedom Trail and the Boston Tea Party were all very interesting, but eventually I had to call a halt. We were working hard and getting tired of being tourists! I started to worry about the 26 mile trip which was the reason I was really out there. Even in the spring and with some rain, Boston was an excellent place to visit, but I didn't want to walk the whole city.

Eating in Boston was also a treat. For some strange reason going out to eat has always been something I have enjoyed. As I recall, Boston was one of the best. One reason we could do the whole Boston thing was that we were both working full time and didn't have any children. The most significant part of the experience was actually a verification of a suspicion. After going out for dinner for the second time and watching my wife eating less that half of her fantastic meal, we decided it must be true that our first child was on the way. Boston in and of it self is special to any runner, but knowing we were headed into parenthood while being there certainly made it something we would never forget.

After two more days of relaxation, it was the day of the race. I wore nothing fancy, an old pair of maroon running shorts and a navy blue t-shirt. My disposable sweats were in place and I had visited with a man from Wisconsin and planned to ride downtown with them. They were a middle aged, fiftyish couple who were infatuated with the whole running thing. They were excellent people, as so many runners seem to be, and they actually helped me to relax. Once we boarded the bus, it seemed like things would be well in hand. For some strange reason that bus ride seemed like the longest ride of my life. With the traffic and going around via the freeway, it was certainly not quick. My pressing thought on that cool, misty morning was that I must be crazy. As long as the bus ride was taking me, there was no way I could actually run that same distance.

We finally arrived in Hopkinton, and as I had read about it, it was definitely a small town. In 1979 there seemed to be enough room for all the runners at the school. You could actually go inside, use a real bathroom with only the usual case of nerves, and wonder whether you really need to go and how many times, and all that goes with pre-race preparation. At one point I was headed for what was apparently an official bathroom facility, and I had the honor of seeing the legend, Josh Stemple, redirecting runners in his gruff, directive manner. I stretched and relaxed for awhile on a small section of the extremely crowded gym floor. Deciding it was time to head to the starting line, I was amazed by how many runners had gathered outside, and saw more people relieving themselves in those next couple of blocks than I had seen in my lifetime! Hopkinton had to be the most urine-soaked town in America on that Monday morning. One of the hedges I jogged past had an entire line of human waterers at work.

The start was really exciting! Luckily it was cool, around 50 degrees, and I was still wearing an extra sweatshirt, one of those all-purpose gray jobbies that I knew would not be with me for long. With the excitement, the crowd, and the feeling of many years of running history that had passed by that same starting line, I proudly began my first Boston Marathon. The first mile is essentially down-hill, and I do recall being quite aggressive, and then catching myself -ah, remember- this is a 26 mile race. I checked my mental clock, eased off a bit, and made my way toward Boston proper. Settling in, I relaxed, felt the body temperature starting to adjust to the work of the day, and with a bit of relief and a feeling of celebration I took the sweatshirt off, spun it in a circle, and through it into the woods.

That day would turn out to be one of those where the weather kind of gets stuck. It never got much warmer, stayed overcast until the rain started a little over half-way. It commonly happens that few details of a marathon race can even be remembered. I recall the fun and excitement of passing through the small Eastern communities. For those who have heard about the women of Wellesley College, it is all true. They were noisy, screaming, jumping up and down and very inspiring. I was not as inspired as the gentlemen next to me who dropped to the street and did several pushups for them, but I was inspired. I had run up "heartbreak hill" a couple of days before, so I knew what to expect, and it really wasn't that big of a thing. It is actually a series of three hills that occur at a terrible place in the course, like miles 19 and 20. Their size and intimidation were not to be a part of this old cross country runner's problems, but just rather one more thing to survive. I had spent a good deal of time training on local hills back home to get ready for the race. Evidently my preparation was better than some because several people were really struggling, some were slowly jogging, and some were choosing to walk up parts of the hills. A bigger problem that I recall was the downhill stretch of cobble-stone street a little beyond "heartbreak." That was where I felt the pain the most, and my sensitive muscles and feet were really complaining. Those who have run a few long races know the feeling. It seems strange that downhill running should cause the most pain, but sometimes it really hurts. The old wish came to mind, "Feet, Don't Fail me Now!"

The feet didn't fail, the body didn't fail. Exhausted, dripping from the rain, and being several hundred miles from home, I became a finisher of the Boston Marathon. The feeling was fantastic, the race had gone according to plan, but I was shot. Almost an hour prior, somewhere around mile seventeen, I heard word of the first people finishing. For myself, for my goals, for my thinking, I was every bit as much of a winner as I needed to be. I had set a goal, made a plan, trained for months, and concluded with my fastest marathon to date, 2:46:15. Now, where the heck was my wife? I wandered around the parking ramp area, sat for a bit, walked for a bit, and headed to the motel lobby where we had agreed to meet. True to form, I didn't find her, but she found me, and she had more of a story to share than I did. While walking downtown Boston about an hour before the race started, she was visiting with someone and was told if she wanted to see the finish she needed to get there now. It was already raining in downtown Boston at the start of the race, so she proceeded to stand in the rain (with our new umbrella), for four hours just to see me finish. Luckily, after seeing 2,142 others finish she did happen to look up and witness the fact that I did cross the line. There were 7,977 runners that finished the race that day, but she didn't watch the rest of them. I guess this drowned rat of a wasted runner was enough for her on that drizzly day in April of 1979.

I don't recall how long we stayed in the area, but before long we headed to the subway station. My wife kept asking me how I was doing and I just replied that if we walked slowly I'd be fine. We found our stop and paid, only a quarter or thirty-five cents at that time, and we made our way down the subway stairs. Of course, the Boston Marathon always is held on a state holiday, Patriots Day, and the whole state and the whole city of Boston is on vacation Needless to say, the subway was packed. We are not exactly world travelers, and making connections and getting to the right spot can be stressful on a normal day. So, there we were standing in the subway, hanging on to one of those hooks they provide for keeping your balance and we swayed around curves and stopped and started with mildly abrupt movements. At this point, I start to lose it. A little dizzy, a little woozy, and being a six foot guy staring downward at the ladies hat in front of me, I panicked. "Honey, we have got to get off this subway!" She said something like, "What,? Right here in the middle of nowhere? We don't even know where we are!" At that point it didn't matter; I needed to leave or the alternative was going to be emptying whatever was in my stomach right over that poor, short, little lady with her quaint maroon hat. Well, we got off, took a fifteen minute break, and eventually got back on to finish our ride out to Cambridge. It had been a beautiful daily walk past the Harvard Campus to our motel, but it was a little slower on that particular Monday afternoon. I never did get sick, but just needed some adjustment time to get normal again.

As I recap this experience today, it was, indeed, unique and rewarding. I could have come up with several reasons not to go: it will cost a lot of money or I'll miss work, but these are not good reasons. Runners need to find ways to do the special things that will make running more complete. Without a doubt, one of the most significant ways I have done just that in my life was by running in the Boston Marathon.

Lesson learned: There are some great running events in our country, and you might find the experience very interesting and gratifying if you can find a way to be a part of one of those awesome happenings.

07

ADULT JOB - FOLLOWING THE CAREER PATH

After using up four years of college running eligibility and acquiring 100 extra college credits, there was only one thing left to do: get a diploma. Luckily college wasn't too expensive in the seventies and nice jobs seemed to come my way. I didn't have any loans to pay back, and I was able to pull a 4.0 for the first time in my last quarter of classes. I had majors in Physical Education and Health Education, a minor in Biology, and certifications in both Driver's Training and Athletic Coaching. However, I still honestly did not know what I was going to do. I had changed areas of study from music, to biology, to English, and then ended up with the above mentioned majors. The final spring competitive season had resulted in more positive running experiences. The leadership roles of captain for both teams and an officer of the lettermen's club helped shape my poise and confidence. We had a very good final season in track and field, now it was time for the last obligation to graduate, student teaching.

The fall of our fifth year, my room-mate and I decided to do our student teaching in the Twin Cities. That experience is what decided which direction my professional life would be going. I had a great experience at North St. Paul and about six weeks into it, I was spending the evening at school for an open house. Lots of people attended, and there was an open gym along with the evening activity. I was spending some time bouncing on a trampoline, not the small circular ones of today but an official competitive rectangular competitive apparatus. (Sometimes it really is too bad that in today's society law suits and paranoia seem to abound. As a result, many activities that most people use responsibly, like the trampoline, have been taking away.) Anyway, that particular evening is when my brain had a complete revelation, and I knew I wanted to be a teacher and a coach! I suppose the idea had been circling around in my brain for quite awhile, but on that night it became a certainty for me. I actually knew what I wanted to do, and it felt great. One more unique thing about student teaching was that I became the Head Junior High Cross Country Coach along with my practice teaching. There had been some mental complications affecting the previous coach, and a science teacher agreed to tag along and make things legal if I would be the coach. The coaching worked out well, the teaching was going great, and I became excited about what I wanted to do with the rest of my life.

Unfortunately, when student teaching came to an end, I had car payments that I had deferred and I didn't have a job. I felt obligated to go back to my home town and work as a used water pump inspector. After six weeks I was very, very fortunate to be able to escape that profession, and I secured a position teaching K-8 Physical Education part time in Minneapolis. Along with substitute teaching for Minneapolis Public Schools, I was able to easily pay the bills, and I started writing letters of application for full-time teaching positions. Computers were just coming out in 1976, so I spent many hours typing away on some cheap typewriter. I sent letters everywhere. Much to my amazement my college town hired me, and I was heading back to Bemidji, Minnesota, as a teacher instead of a student.

I was young, a little crazy, very enthusiastic, and I immediately had year-round coaching in Cross Country, Swimming, and Track and Field. A lot of that training, coaching, and running with my athletes resulted in my running the Boston Marathon as described in Mile 6.. My athletes inspired me, and I in turn must have inspired them, because we had some excellent success. All of my coaching at first was junior high or on the assistant varsity level. During the spring of 1980, I coached my first state-placed winner to a third place finish. The following spring I had the honor of coaching a double state champion. I had actually been his eighth grade coach and had converted him from the hurdles to distance running, probably still one of the smartest moves of my career. At sub-regions in his senior year, Brian Kraft and I successfully trained, and he executed a great race plan to win the 1600 meter run in a time of 4:15.9. There really was no one that could stay close to him at the first level of tournament competition, so we made a very specific plan to simply run fast. His record still stands in our high school today. He also ran 9:13.7 for two miles, another record that is still his. At the state championships he ran the two mile the first day and out-powered the field in the last lap to become the Minnesota State Champion in that event. As we cooled down together, we were both ecstatic and spent some quiet time jogging together through the residential neighborhood outside the venue. After discussing the race and being thrilled together, I let him know that our work was not over. I had all the confidence in the world to think he could repeat the next day and win the mile too. The taper was working beautifully, and he was healthy and extremely strong. He accepted the idea that the next day could be equally as great, and he promised me he would do his best.

The next day was sunny, a beautiful fresh spring day at a little over 70 degrees and the mile race was in the middle of the afternoon. The state meet was done in such a way that on the first day of competition, usually a Friday, the larger schools competed separately from the smaller schools. The second day they brought everyone together for the finals, racing the relays, qualifiers in the dashes, and the mile on Saturday. It was quite an atmosphere and the crowd really supported the runners. This was the first year in Minnesota that athletes were allowed to double in the one mile and two mile. Our division, the boy's large-school race, was the fourth mile race of the day. The small-school race of girls and boys went first, followed by the large-school girls' race. Now it was time for us to step back on the track. It was a typical start with everyone bunched and being a little conservative the first two laps. At the start of lap three, Brian and two other runners started to move out and leave the pack behind. Luckily things were going mostly as we had expected. It is often the case that the pace is not blistering and tactics are employed. The three runners in front had established themselves as the state's fastest, and they were making their move. At the start of the straight-away going into the end of lap three, Brian was in third and he was running between the two leaders, just a half stride behind them. At this point I feared he might get disqualified. He made a bold step between the two runners, and with 500 meters to go went into a fantastic kick that buried them both and earned another Minnesota State Track and Field Championship. It was an awesome finish to a great high school career, and his performances fell right into his master plan, which was to wait to commit to a college until after the state meet. These two fantastic races would make him very marketable, and I was extremely pleased to help him reach this level of excellence.

Nine months prior to that double state championship, I started the first Girls' Cross Country team at Bemidji High School. The 1980-81 school year was a big year for me, and, oh yes, they did not pay me to coach that first fall. I volunteered, even though I was doing all the same work (and probably more) as the head boys' coach. My pay that year was the conference trophy the girls won, the many happy looks on their faces, and the thanks of the girls and their parents for giving them the opportunity. Looking back, this was a very big event in the history of Bemidji High School. It began a new sport that provided another opportunity for many girls and a successful program from its inception. I was not looking to make history or to be a martyr that insisted on starting the program no matter what. Several of the girls and their families approached me, and I just saw it as something that was "right" to do. Sue Bonovich had pioneered the effort the previous year by being the only girl competing for cross country, running with the boys' coaches and an entire team of boys. She often would ask me if I thought it was worth her effort, and if it was really good for her to be doing what she was doing. I simply encouraged her and told her to relax, run, and not worry about all those other things. She did have a great, positive personality and I definitely saw more smiles than frowns coming from her that season. Isn't that the real beauty of what running is all about?

Our new group of girls loved a challenge and they had already established a love for life on the run. They were a pleasant group and were willing to work hard. We did find some early success and their "nothing to lose" attitude served them well. They also came to believe in themselves as a team and that is why they were able to be conference champions as a first year team. It certainly helped that we had ten runners right from the start and they all completed that entire first season. Here is a copy of my paycheck for that first coaching job:

The following spring the current head coach of Cross Country and Track decided to visit with me one day as we walked out to the track. He informed me he was going to teach for one more year and then become an administrator and that this would be his last spring of coaching. Due to those fine successes the previous year, I was in the right spot at the right time. The other assistant and I decided that I would be head Cross Country Coach of both boys and girls, he would be head boy's Track Coach, and we would assist each other. The school district agreed, and we began an awesome tradition of running success at our school.

B.K., Brian Kraft's initials, is what I have called these writings for the past several years. He is important as to why running came to mean so much to me. He loved running and, by what you have read here and will read later, his love for running was extremely important for his entire life. He did obtain a very lucrative scholarship to Missouri and was set for a brilliant college career, or so we thought.

Lesson learned: Believe in yourself, and approach new things with confidence and a positive attitude.

HOMETOWN MARATHON, BEMIDJI, MINNESOTA, 1981

"The thrill is not just in winning, but in the courage to join the race!"

Outside my elementary gymnasium a poster used to hang on the wall that made the above statement. It was, I suppose, the essence of my vocation. Thousands of kids have been active and hopefully have remained active through my teaching of Physical Education and coaching of Cross Country and Track and Field. Winning was fine, losing was fine, but doing our best was what was always important. Just doing the activity at all was important. It does take courage, we won't always like it, but the gain, the reason, and the benefit comes from a positive attitude and a willingness to "join the race".

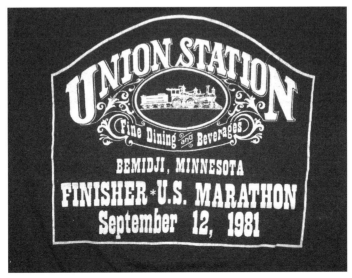

(The shirt is a little deceptive, as you will learn in this chapter this was not a marathon where I was able to cross the finish line. Being a race in my hometown, I knew the race director well. The race ended up being a one-year event so I am glad I was a part of it. They knew I had worked harder than probably anyone else who ran that day to get ready for the race, and they insisted I have one of the shirts.)

Union Station Marathon, Bemidji, Minnesota

During 1981 time was a concept of which I did not have much to spare. I worked full-time, coached many hours a week, and tried to be a caring husband and father of two little ones. I had also become the head coach for two sports and a very involved coach in the third program. Wow, there must have been a high score on the crazy scale up there somewhere. Oh well, I've done crazy things before! This year I had trained once again at the level of questionable sanity, 100 miles a week for the third and fourth weeks prior to a marathon. This marathon was a local race in the years when our city thought they could support such an activity as a full-fledged marathon. I hoped I was ready for a great performance. Many of my local athletes worked at the race or drove around in their parents' cars trying to cheer on the masses attempting to run 26 miles. Most of them were primarily cheering for me, their coach.

After experiencing several marathons I suppose I should have known better. Ah yes, the old problem, which shoes to wear. (It is safe to say I always have several to choose from.) The particular pair I chose to wear for the race had only about three weeks of wear, but they felt so good! A couple of easy, enjoyable, well cushioned ten milers convinced me they were the pair to wear. Oh my, ten miles does not a marathon make. Reaching the six mile mark of a marathon should be a piece of cake. Well actually it was, but between mile six and mile seven my foot, or more correctly my toes of my right foot, started the slow burn. It was just an aggravation, a hot spot, something that would now be a part of my day, and it would be there for every step I would take. The pain was gradually grasping more and more of my focus with each agonizing mile, reluctantly I began to examine the options. My thrust became to make it to my house which was close to the fifteen mile mark. I planned to change into my favorite training shoe; and things would "certainly" work out and I would be able finish.

Those first fifteen miles were around our beautiful lake which I have circled many times. On a normal day it would be an awesome run which includes a two mile section through our state park. I have enjoyed many runs there in the past. I have even raced the 25k around the lake several times with some nice success. With what seemed like way too much effort, I made it to that 15 mile mark, grabbed the relief pair of shoes out of the closet, and got back on the course. Granted things were not smooth, and it was one of those overly warm days that my body has personally never enjoyed, but I was back on the road. The first two miles seemed better at first, as my toes weren't quite so uncomfortable, but the relief was only temporary. Soon the problem became not an aggravation but a dinosaur living inside my shoe. When I reached a highway bypass bridge, I knew I had to take a realistic look at the situation. I sat down, the sun shining more than I would have liked, and realized I smelled like an overworked animal that had covered nineteen laborious miles. I slowly took off my shoe and peeled off my sock. Oops!! Out of the side of my second toe which was longer than my big toe, there appeared a repetitive, pulsing, clear liquid shooting out of my foot. Having a graduate degree in health education, I knew this was not normal, and I accepted the fact that the day was indeed done. Ah well, not the first disappointment of a lifetime runner, and probably not the last. The choice wasn't difficult, but facing the clean up of telling family, team, and friends would prove to be the harder thing to do.

How far should a middle age life time runner train for things like marathons and road races? I can honestly say that was the last time I spent that much time and number of miles training for a race. Training at the 100 mile per week level took a lot of organization! Especially with my busy career, a growing family, and my wife also worked full time. I guess you could say my wife must have believed in me, because I cannot imagine how else she allowed me to attack my running to that magnitude.

Making sense of training, and what is necessary to accomplish individual goals, means different things to different people. Somehow, through it all, I have come to believe that those that run the furthest perform the best. I would admit this philosophy is not true for everyone, but it has been what works for me and a majority of the young people I have worked with. A basic responsibility of running a marathon does have to do with acceptance of what your body can endure on any given day. That particular hometown marathon day wasn't so enjoyable, but I'm still pleased I made the effort and had the courage to join the race.

There is another marathon in north central Minnesota that enjoys a lot more success than the Bemidji race did. It is the Walker North Country Marathon in the beautiful resort community of Walker, Minnesota. It is an October race and it also has a half marathon, a half marathon relay, and a 10k along with it. This marathon has also been a one time experience for me, although I have raced the 10k several times.

On a beautiful October morning in 1998, I drove thirty-six miles to the south to run the North Country Marathon. The early morning temperature was in the mid-fifties. The small field of runners was a hearty looking bunch and they were excited to begin a 26 mile trek that included several miles of trail running. The downhill start was a good reminder for me to not get overly excited and be conservative, allowing myself to make the entire loop of 26 miles. The goal was to get my body all the way around the loop and back to where we started from.

For the first couple of miles we enjoyed the great scenery provided by the shores of Leech Lake. We even ran over a small bridge that had water on both sides of it. It provided an extremely cool view of our northern Minnesota lake country. As we eventually made a right turn and headed south, going further down the highway, trees flanked the road and I anticipated the turn into the forest trail.

I hit the trail with a huge amount of enthusiasm. We had gone seven miles and the highway had become a bit boring. The trail was narrow, but the trees provided shade and the thick forest swallowed us up and changed our running style. I actually whooped with joy as we began that part of the course. I have always loved trails and woods running. After three miles of the trail, and ten miles of total running, I had a different thought and revelation. There wasn't any flat ground anywhere in the woods! We were constantly running downhill, uphill, slanting to the right or slanting to the left. This became very stressful as the miles started to add up and I knew the difficult course would add several minutes on to my expected marathon time.

After several miles winding through the woods we finally crossed a gravel road and then commenced to come out on the next gravel road. From there we did a short gravel loop and ended up on an old railroad bed trail. By the time I reached that point the temperature had climbed into the high sixties and I was completely exhausted. The sun was beating straight down and the thick trees flanking the trail no longer provided any extra cooling effect. I had been drinking water, but it wasn't helping, and I continued getting more uncomfortable by the mile. I had not taken in any other replacement fluids. I stopped at the aid station, probably at about the twenty mile mark, and I had serious doubts as to whether I would be finishing the race. I drank four nice glasses of their energy drink, and it worked wonders. As I started down the completely flat trail I started to feel like I actually did have a little more energy. The miles remarkably became do-able and I felt those four glasses of energy replacement were primarily why I made it to the finish line. It wasn't real pretty, especially when there was a huge five-block uphill climb right before the finish. But, I did make it up the hill, crossed the road onto the high school track, and finished in front of the grand stand. This was the first time I experienced having a fluid replacement drink affect whether or not I actually finished a race. The country side had been beautiful, and it had been great to run in the woods, but the energy output was huge. I was grateful I could replace my depletion with enough nutrients to help me find the finish line. There have been times when I have run 26 miles while taking very little liquids at the aid stations, but that day in Walker, Minnesota taught my how important they really can be.

This marathon is probably the most connected race ever as far as community support. Many non running people, who are great fans, help to make this race happen every year. The race is a very well-established event. Besides being a very unique resort area in which to run 26 miles, it is a fun place to spend the day! I would encourage anyone to experience it, but just remember it is more of a trail run than a regular marathon. Their race theme is "A Celebration of the Life and Land that is Northern Minnesota".

Lesson learned: Hydration and fuel replacement are VERY important to being successful at running the marathon.

PAAVO NURMI MARATHON, HURLEY, WISCONSIN, 1985

What is Paavo Nurmi anyway?

Our neighbor state of Wisconsin has a northern marathon in the town of Hurley, Wisconsin. It is right across the river from Michigan and a nice, cozy place for a summer marathon. The race is named after a famous Finnish distance runner, therefore, there is quite a faction of Finns in the community, with the race being a very social affair.

My first experience there was in the summer of 1972 with the same group of college guys who participated in the Atlanta Marathon. We all literally "trucked" over there in my buddy's father's pickup truck. There were four of us and it was just sort of on a whim that we decided to enter the Paavo Nurmi Marathon. The spaghetti feed at that time was in a local, old church and the townspeople actually opened up their homes to the athletes, putting us up for the night. One friend we called "Philly" had entered us and set everything up, so we decided to head up there and have a good time. I had been doing some limited cross country training but nothing close to what I needed for a marathon.

We located our host family and introduced ourselves, determined sleeping arrangements, then headed out for a little shake out jog to get the ride out of our systems. After a mile of easy running we stretched, went back to our host's home and got ready for the spaghetti feed. It was a small, quaint affair at that time, and after dinner we headed back to try and get some rest for an eight o'clock race start.

The next morning, I was running along fine for quite awhile until around mile twelve when my high inner thigh, in other words the crotch area, became immensely aggravated. At times like this, running can get very personal. Our running group had become experienced veterans of Vaseline usage and methods of trying to prevent foot and body chafing problems, but of all days, this one wasn't going well for me. By mile fourteen, I headed into the woods and found a private place to take off my jock strap and throw it away. Obviously, this was a country race which involved a couple of small towns but primarily rolling hills through the wooded area of northern Wisconsin. So there I was, looking all around to find a secluded spot to do my thing. I finished my business, and gingerly stepped back onto the tar road of the race course. Once again I failed on that day. Giving it the old college try, I made it to mile seventeen, saw this beautiful lake off to the right, and simply dove in and called it a day. My training was just getting started for the September season, and I had been working full time, so I guess the cards were not really stacked in my favor. However, the buddies and I had a good time. We drove to Superior, Wisconsin, had a great night dancing and consuming that favorite beverage of some marathoners, and ended the evening with all four of us sleeping in the pickup camper. Experiences like that makes a group of college team members really close after four years together.

Somehow I again chose to go back there in 1974, with even less training and try it again. This time a home town buddy of mine, a baseball player, decided to go along, and he entered the race too. He had not trained at all. Well, he made it to the nine mile mark and called it a day while I made it fourteen miles this time. The real reason why you might ask? It was 88 degrees at eight o'clock in the morning! The run is usually held on the first weekend of August, but that year it was by far the hottest temperature ever. We basically spent the weekend at an area motel and enjoyed the area. We chalked our running up to experience, or the lack of it. I will say my friend Tom really enjoyed the effort and was very proud he had made it nine miles.

After two failures, I later convinced my supportive wife in 1985 that we should take a trip to a place I'd visited a couple of times, and that I thought the family would enjoy. We now had three children, and the wild man wanted to run the marathon again. This time I thought I had done the training for it, and I would be going back to conquer the course. Maybe it was maturity or just plain being stubborn, but I wanted to think that a marathon course could not get the best of me. Our first night was most interesting. We had our camping gear along, and we decided to sleep in a small campground in the neighboring town across the river in Michigan. We settled in the cute, homey Ironwood Campground, hiked, played on the playground, had a simple meal complete with s'mores, and settled in for the evening. The five of us slept together in one small tent, our one, four and five-year-old children snug in their sleepers. It was actually a very peaceful evening, and we had a good night of rest. I woke up early and decided to open up the fly on the tent a bit and check out the day. Oh no, things in the sky did not look good! There was a huge storm coming in fast from the west and I knew we didn't have much time. My wife and I quickly got dressed. We gently threw the kids and all our gear in the car, and immediately left the campground. The sprinkles started as I jumped in the car and it was a complete downpour before we got out the driveway of the campground. I knew there was a nice breakfast spot right down the road towards Hurley, so we drove there to wait out the storm. I stopped right in front of the door and helped my family inside. The restaurant people were very nice and fully understood our situation, so we had a nice calm morning breakfast, the kids still in their sleepers, while the thunder, lightning, and rain roared all around. Somehow the coffee never tasted so good, and I was really happy my family was safe and mostly dry.

We decided that was enough of camping and after a few phone calls and questions, I reserved a nice two story condominium for a very reasonable price. The area was big on winter activities such as snowmobiling and skiing and it was easy to get a good price for a room in August. The night before the race we again attended the pre-race dinner at the old church, and after a good night's sleep in the condo, it was time to get up and start Paavo Nurmi Marathon #3.

The weather on race day was much more reasonable, a warm day but not a scorcher. I believe it was about sixty degrees at race start, and it never got really warm. I was determined to leave the small town where the race began, tour the country on leg power, and arrive in downtown Hurley. I really didn't want to rely on any motorized vehicle to help me get back into town. There were 282 people entered in the race, but I spent way too much time dealing with one particular runner. This interesting guy's running strategy went against all of my personal running beliefs and ideals. His approach to racing revolved around an alternating approach where he would go hard for a mile and then walk the next mile. The only problem was I hooked up with this guy at about mile five, and for the next twelve miles we were stuck on a ridiculous pattern. During his fast mile he would pass me and go out ahead, and during the next mile I would pass him in return. I really am a quite amiable person, and I usually try to figure anybody has the right to do things their own way. But after doing this back and forth for an awfully long time it really started to bother me. Luckily, I was very focused and things were working well, and I was having a good day. When we reached mile seventeen, I continued to keep my steady pace as I passed him for the last time. He seemed to be laboring, and at last he was no longer able to catch me. Thankfully, our time spent together was finally over.

The course was entirely small paved roads, with a fair amount of turns and a moderate amount of hills. I was able to continue running strong as I passed the woods near the fourteen mile mark where I had shed the jock strap years ago. I had now solved that problem with wearing half tights under my shorts, making the run much more comfortable. In the same mile I had previously had my lake plunge, I was able to acknowledge the beautiful water and continue down the road, still feeling strong. Somehow I had acquired the mental manipulation of using natural things such as sunshine and water to give me strength and confidence. After leaving the lake I was determined to make it to one particular point on the course. Every time I had been to Hurley, I had driven the course before I tried to race it. There is a big, steep, uphill, about a third of a mile long, which leads the runners back into town. It is somewhat ironic that this uphill obstacle occurs at about mile twenty-two and runs parallel to a large cemetery. Between the road and the cemetery loom huge trees and many large, eerie tombstones. My goal was to reach that hill and run it being strong. Some say the third time is a charm and indeed this time it was. I was checking my watch, still passing some other runners, as I crested the hill feeling fine and headed for the finish line. Hearing the sounds of "Yeah Daddy" and "Way to go" I finally found the finish line of the Paavo Nurmi Marathon. My time was three hours and one minute, just slightly faster than a seven minute per mile average, and I was very, very pleased. I had finished 32nd out of 282 runners entered. I had also found what I considered to be a large amount of success on the roads of Wisconsin.

We hung around the small town for awards and a light lunch because by now we were all hungry. My prize was a belt buckle and I was proud to have earned it. We found a typical small town eating and drinking establishment and just sat down to relax and wind down. This time I felt fine and really enjoyed some quiet time with my family after successfully getting to another marathon finish line. After 45 minutes or so I had to use the bathroom, so I headed in there and pulled up to the urinal. What a concept: the outlook from that perspective was a see-through wall which allowed you to look into the outer hallway while you did your business. Of course, I had to tell my family what I had experienced and took the time to show my five-year-old son the view. He really thought that was funny.

Lesson learned: A negative situation at one point in your life, does not need to be the same way the next time around. Commitment , maturity and dedication can lead to success. Keep looking forward to new and better days.

10

TWIN CITIES MARATHON, MINNEAPOLIS, MINNESOTA, 1984

A special aspect of Minnesota running, that thousands of runners have been a part of over the years is our two famous marathons. One ranking I have seen claims that Grandma's Marathon in Duluth, Minnesota, and the Twin Cities Marathon connecting Minneapolis and St. Paul, are two of the top ten marathons in the United States. Both are events that I honestly cherish, and I know many runners have appreciated the experience of being involved in them. Over the years I have always read about them, occasionally watched them, and of course I have also been a participant in them.

During my first teaching job, I spent a short time living in Minneapolis. I have always had relatives there, and being a lifetime Minnesotan, I have attended many events in the area. Even though I felt I knew a lot about the Twin Cities area, I was delightfully shocked with how well they put together the race course for the TC Marathon.

The Twin Cities Marathon is called the "most beautiful urban marathon" in their registration materials, and it honestly is that great. The trees, the parks, water, bridges, and overall feel the race course gives you as you run between the cities of Minneapolis and St. Paul, is really special. Perhaps the fresh air of October in Minnesota is an additional positive benefit, but the whole experience is unique. It is also a great atmosphere for first-time marathoners. I would encourage anyone interested in running the race to go ahead and enter it, odds are quite high that you will have a great run. The fans and interested supporters are very understanding and they seem to really value the idea of all of the runners having a positive experience.

The year was 1984 and the three of us had trained as a group. We had spent months getting ready to spend that October day in the Twin Cities. We signed up for the race together and it would be the first time running that course for all of us. I have trained with lots of people over the years, but these two guys are the ones I have trained with the most. One was along on that initial run that started this book and the other one will be a part of a Boston story yet to come. One was also that coach who I initially split up coaching positions with, and one was my original teaching partner in my school district. Years of training, planning, racing and learning to love life on the run brought us to this race together.

The course began in downtown Minneapolis in the shadows of the Metrodome (the recent home of the Minnesota Twins and the current home for the Minnesota Vikings). A clear, crisp, fall morning in the largest city in our state, made the start very exciting. The hype, the anticipation, the excitement all quickly became a big part of that beautiful day. I don't recall if we were together on the starting line, but I know in a short period of time I was out ahead of both of them. I have always been a little extra assertive at the start of races and have never feared getting out there and seeing what the day has to offer. I would guess they chose to begin the race together in a more conservative mode. Because it was a cool forty-two degree morning, I actually started the run in a maroon, long sleeved turtle neck.

During the first part of the race I was aggressive, but definitely under control. Within a few blocks of running through the downtown area, we came to the first of several lakes, a small clear lake, lined with park benches, birds, and walkways. Most Minnesotans would probably call it a pond. It was picturesque and it bordered the southwest corner of downtown. From there we wound through a peripheral area of downtown and a little after mile three the field of runners came to a nice, enjoyable series of larger lakes. The running path was a mixture of tarred parkway roads and tarred trails that surrounded the lakes area and continued for another five miles. When we left the beautiful lakes area we entered the area known as Minnehaha Parkway. This part of the course had more mature trees and there was grass all around as we ran through a very pleasant housing area. The crowd in this area was huge and very festive. Finishing the parkway we reached the mighty Mississippi at mile fifteen. At that point we turned north, and we were still provided more protection from the sun by huge trees on the banks of the Mississippi River.

My pace was strong and I was moving well, quite a bit under seven minutes a mile. I was doing "Barny" running math as I ran from one mile to the next. When I heard or saw my mile time I automatically added seven minutes to that time. My goal was to remember that new time and just stay loose and smooth and try to get to the next mile mark under that number. Of course the idea was to adjust up or down with my speed if I didn't get the time I was looking for. Things like hills or adopting a different runner's pace sometimes caused the time to be faster or slower, but this method helped me maintain my rhythm. It also gave me a bit of an external focus, and it was helping me to believe that my training had provided me with an adequate amount of preparation. The numbers kept giving me a high level of confidence, and things were feeling very good. I tried to be efficient, looking at my watch only once, just as I passed the mile mark. I made quick mental notes of how that mile had gone, and then added the seven minutes to clarify the next goal. I didn't dwell on the individual result for that mile. I simply made a mental note of it, calculated the next projected mile time, and adjusted my rhythm and pace accordingly. It was a motivating way to continue receiving positive feedback. I was hitting my splits well, often quite a few seconds below seven minutes per mile.

One goal for the day was to run at my goal pace and try to maintain that for the entire race. I tried to do that in a way that I continually stayed in my comfort zone. The feeling I was trying to obtain was one of somewhat holding back and waiting to let it go. I would be picking a spot from which I would decide to be aggressive all the way to the end. All during miles sixteen and seventeen I was definitely having that feeling. I felt that I could go faster, but I had some concerns because the weather was starting to heat up. I was still wearing the long sleeved turtle neck. The temperature had climbed into the fifties, and I was spending quite a bit of time deciding when to dump the shirt. As I crossed the Franklin Avenue Bridge and I had covered a little over nineteen miles, I met my wife. She had a different pair of shoes for me, but I told her my feet where doing fine. I gave her my shirt and it felt great to leave it behind. She had a lighter shirt waiting for me, but I just elected to not bother to take it. Most guys weren't running with bare chests that day, but that felt really comfortable to me. Meeting my wife with additional clothing had all been planned. I knew I might be running without a shirt. At that time we were identified only with our race numbers and not timing chips, so my number was pinned to my running shorts. All this took just a few seconds, and I decided to change my pace and start to pick it up a little.

From there the course headed south down the East River Road. We were now on the opposite side of the Mississippi River. The entire boulevards on either side of the river were lined will tall, mature, hard wood trees that provided continual shade and very enjoyable scenery. As a matter of fact, on the east side the river was on our right, but on the left side most of the houses were actually mansions. The beautifully manicured lawns and gardens were a pleasant distraction from some other things my mind was telling me. This area was filled with enthusiastic people on both sides of the road. The road was lined with fans, friends, family, and an occasional individual or group providing music. This all helped to keep weary runners moving down the road. I happily ran past a mansion that I was familiar with. My aunt used to work as the head cook for the president of the University of Minnesota. All those very nice things could serve as a distraction, but I maintained my focus and made the left turn to leave the river behind. Most of the runners, including myself, had now made it through another major portion of the course and we had recently passed the twenty-one mile mark.

We were now leaving the many miles of running near the lakes and the river, and beginning our long, final trek down prestigious Summit Avenue. This section has a road down the middle with grass corridors on both sides and an additional side road that has direct access to block after block of beautiful, old elite and expensive homes. Some of these houses would also fit in the mansion category, including the one that houses our Minnesota governor. The straight four miles of running with a couple of very small, gradual up hills on Summit was a time to continue to increase or at least maintain my marathon pace. I knew I was going to complete the race and it was time to get intentional about my finish. I was very fortunate to continually pass people during those last miles and I knew my pace was getting faster. As I headed toward the final huge left turn that goes around the Catholic Cathedral I was entertaining thoughts of breaking 2:50. From that big turn that goes around the beautiful church, you get a downhill look at the State Capitol grounds of St. Paul, Minnesota, and more importantly, the finish line. After leaving Minneapolis, running on all the parkways and around the lakes, running along the mighty Mississippi and then cruising through four miles of old, character filled mansions, you now come to one of the most beautiful finishes any marathon has to offer. By this time in the race you have already been running past hundreds of spectators for all 26 miles, and you are now being encouraged by the huge crowd of people who have come out to see the finish of the Twin Cities' Marathon.

I continued to finish hard and moved smoothly down the final hill to the finish line. It was one of those days when the down hill didn't really bother my legs and there was no problem getting to and over the finish line. One little reward they gave the runners, besides the beautiful finisher's medal, was the huge tin foil type wrap around that really worked well to maintain my body heat. I wrapped it around my bare shoulders and back. That was really comforting as I was waiting to link up with my clothes. I was extremely pleased that I was able to finish the Twin Cities tour in two hours, fifty-one minutes, and fifteen seconds. I was 324th out of 4,400 runners. My buddies were also both under three hours and we had a very good day! We joined many others in enjoying a wonderful running experience together and we relaxed on the beautiful grassy lawn that was just slightly downhill from the Minnesota State Capitol.

The entire course and the experience was positive and I was personally surprised how well the race had gone. My training had provided for a great day. I knew I had completed an extreme effort and that felt really good. My race plan worked well and I had delightfully been able to run faster than my goal had been for the day. I could not stop thinking of how truly enjoyable they had designed the marathon course. After months of preparation, I was very happy to have had the experience, it was really a good day on the run. After getting back to the in-laws, a short distance from the finish area, I spent several calming minutes in Grandma's whirlpool tub. It was great for a little relaxation, reflection, and a few moments to evaluate and appreciate the great day.

The three of us at the finish area of Twin Cities Marathon.

Lesson learned: Large metropolitan marathons can be a very enjoyable experience. The Twin Cities put together all the cool things the two cities had to offer, and the fans were very supportive.

11

SPECIAL TIMES AT TWIN CITIES MARATHON

Taking runners from Minneapolis to St. Paul, the Twin Cities Marathon has come to mean a lot to me. My first teaching job was about four miles from one part of the marathon course, and my wife's family still lives about four miles from the finish line. One of my first road races was on that same Summit Avenue that makes up the last four mile straight away on the marathon course. I have run other races on various parts of the course, including my first Boston qualifier, at that time called the City of Lakes Marathon. The course went around two of the same Minneapolis lakes and it was the precursor to what is now the Twin Cities Marathon.

One very special event took place on that same marathon course in 2005 when our daughter finished the first marathon of her life. She was a good high school runner, an even better college runner, and she had certainly come to value a healthy lifestyle that involved running. She finished the Twin Cities Marathon in four hours and ten minutes. The goal was simply to finish the race, and she was very pleased to find her first marathon finish line. The usual thoughts were part of her day. I ran some of miles fifteen to twenty-two with her. She was mad at her feet feeling hot and just wanted to run the last part barefooted, but she stopped and hugged several friends and support personnel along the way. Other college friends and metro runners were also making their way to the finish line. The group had met up before the race and had made arrangements to all meet afterwards on that same Capitol lawn mentioned in Mile 10. Her mother and I were both there to encourage her and very pleased to give her a huge hug after finishing the race. As her team mates gathered together after the race, and time was getting a little long, the last two of their social group finally joined them. They were looking extremely happy for just finishing 26 miles, probably due to the fact that the guy had somehow carried an engagement ring for the whole race, and he presented it to his new fiancée at the finish line. The salty, limping, tired group proceeded to exchange many hugs of congratulations, because they were all obviously sharing a very special day together.

Another significant experience at the Twin Cities Marathon was also very memorable, but its outcome was as sad and devastating as my daughter's experience had been happy. The double state champion from Mile 7 of this book had run a marathon when he was only sixteen years of age. At that early stage of his life he was able to run two hours and forty-three minutes at Grandma's Marathon. Fresh out of high school in 1981, he ran two hours and thirty-one minutes, also at Grandma's. He purposefully wanted to wait to select a college until after that Minnesota State Championship his senior year. With a 4:15 mile and a 9:13 two mile that was not really a problem; we just had to find someone who still had scholarships available. Brian Kraft received a full-ride to Missouri and headed south to begin his college career. However, during the first winter season of track, he developed a sensitive, bothersome area in his back. Through continued pain and discomfort it was eventually discovered that he had a cancerous growth that had to be removed. His career was cut short and he reluctantly returned to Minnesota. His life became drastically changed by surgeries, treatments, and chemotherapy. He was able to have a brief stint of running at North Dakota State University in Fargo, North Dakota. Unfortunately, his life became a constant battle to deal with the cancer that continued to invade his body.

Eventually, Brian would go through a bone marrow transplant, numerous surgeries, more chemotherapy and radiation treatments. He ran through all of it. He did not run as fast as he had in the days of his youth, but he always did it on the run. Part of his treatment plan took place at the University of Minnesota Medical Facility, and while doing weekly chemotherapy treatments he ran the entire time. He would recuperate for a day or two, spend the rest of the week running every day, running even a few miles right before they pumped more drugs into his body. He was extremely positive during the entire ordeal, completing a college degree in Mathematics at the University of Minnesota while he was receiving medical care at the same facility. His relationship with his doctor was fantastic, and while being one of the most famous cancer specialists in the country, the man somehow became a close personal friend of Brian's. The same attitude that had helped Brian perform as a double state champion, prevailed throughout his battle with cancer. By the fall of 1994 he had lived with cancer for twelve years. When he was down to about half of one lung and missing a segment of the other one, he still decided he had to run the Twin Cities Marathon. We are talking about a very driven individual whose life was simply more meaningful because he ran. His very being was completely intertwined with the fact that he was a runner. One of the many things that motivated him was a thought I had instilled in him during high school. His approach to that final marathon revolved around the saying, "The body achieves what the mind conceives."

The doctor accepted the fact that this was something that was very important to Brian, and he reluctantly granted him permission to run the race. Brian had a wonderful girl-friend who was also extremely supportive. Along with that, he and I had been somewhat in touch throughout his post-high school life, and he wanted me to be with him for the "race." He jumped on the starting line for the Twin Cities Marathon in October of 1994 determined to enjoy that "runner's high," and he was very focused to make it to that finish line in St. Paul. I joined him in the lakes area at about five miles and we ran together on the Twin Cities Marathon course. There I was, a supposedly healthy coach, running along side a former athlete and now a good friend, and he was feeling great. He was aggressive, tenacious, positive, and on-pace to make his goal time of three hours and ten minutes. We clicked along a little over seven minute mile pace, and by mile thirteen I was in trouble. One of my legs was just simply not doing well. I got a nerve problem or a muscle quirk that would not allow me to run with my normal stride, and it was painful. I stayed with him until we reached an early bridge across the Mississippi river, then I embarrassingly told him to take it on his own, and I would meet him on the other side of the river when he came back down. I walked across the bridge and stretched and tried to work things out. Brian did the northern loop and came back down the east side of the river. We hooked up again for about two miles, and it just was not going to work for me. I was favoring one leg and I could just not get comfortable. I told him good luck; he gave me one of his great grins and took off on his own with about four miles to go.

It was October of 1994, and Brian finished the last marathon of his life. He had accomplished his goal, and in a very calculating manner that I feel he had certainly learned from the old coach, he ran it in three hours and nine minutes. It was obvious he was very pleased and he had certainly made history again. While feeling badly for not having run more miles with him that day, I was elated that he was able to experience every step of the Twin Cities Marathon in one of the last years of his life. A short time later he actually acquired another cancerous growth near his heart, and his University doctor was the only person who would dare attempt to remove it. From complications with that and all of his other fourteen years of battling cancer, Brian passed away in the early fall of 1997. Many of us paid tribute to a true veteran of running in a church in the cities and his body was laid to rest in the cemetery back in Bemidji. I am proud to say I had the honor and privilege of being his coach.

Throughout Brian's battle he was usually upbeat and positive. One time he came back to visit after losing all of his body hair due to his cancer treatments. He let me know that the women really liked that. He struggled with the fact that his running pace continued to get slower. At the same time he still always felt running was a great thing. Shortly before he died he would go back to the trails around one of the Minneapolis lakes and try one last attempt at jogging. He fell once early and only made about a five minute jog, but he just had to go there and run one last time. I admired his constant courage, his prevailing positive attitude, and his ability to always maintain a balance in his life.

A TRIBUTE TO BRIAN

(friends requested that I write this for his funeral)

IN TWENTY-ONE YEARS OF COACHING, HE IS THE FASTEST PERSON TO EVER RUN THE STREETS, GOLF COURSES, TRAILS, AND TRACKS OF BEMIDJI, MINNESOTA. HE WAS ALSO ONE OF THE CRAZIEST, MOST ENTHUSIASTIC, DEDICATED AND FUN PEOPLE I HAVE EVER WORKED WITH. HIS "MOVE" TO WIN THE MINNESOTA STATE TRACK AND FIELD MEET WILL NEVER BE FORGOTTEN. WITH A LAP AND A QUARTER TO GO, HE SQUIRTED THROUGH THE TOP TWO RUNNERS AND TOOK OFF- NEVER TO BE CAUGHT AGAIN. AFTER BEING AWARDED A FULL SCHOLARSHIP TO MISSOURI, HIS REAL LIFE BATTLE BEGAN. SHORTLY AFTER ARRIVING THERE THE INITIAL DISCOVERY THAT CANCER HAD INVADED HIS BODY SHOCKED ALL OF US. FOR YEARS HE WOULD FIGHT HIS BATTLE AND RUN, FIGHT AND RUN, FIGHT AND RUN, AND EVEN WITH ONLY A PARTIAL LUNG CAPACITY DUE TO CANCER SURGERY, HE WOULD GO ON. A FEW SHORT YEARS AGO WE WERE RUNNING TOGETHER IN THE TWIN CITIES MARATHON. I, SUPPOSEDLY HEALTHY, HAD TO STOP WITH A LEG CRAMP, BUT BRIAN RAN ON, THOUGH SLOWER THAN HIS DAYS OF OLD, TO DO HIS THING AND FINISH THE 26 MILE RACE.

THE RACE WAS GOOD, THE RACE MADE A DIFFERENCE. HE FOUGHT THE GOOD FIGHT WITH CLASS, OBJECTIVITY, AND DETERMINATION. NOW THE FINAL STEP HAS BEEN TAKEN, HE'LL GASP FOR BREATHE NO MORE, AND WE REMEMBER, WE CHERISH, AND WE HONOR A GREAT GUY. HE WAS SOMEONE THAT MANY OF US WILL NEVER BE ABLE TO FORGET. WHEN WE DO A MORNING RUN, WHEN WE RECALL HIS COY SMILE OR HIS LAUGH, WHEN WE REMEMBER THE GOOD TIMES, WHEN WE GO BACK TO THE TWIN CITIES MARATHON, WHEN WE LOOK AT THE BEMIDJI HIGH SCHOOL RECORD BOOK- WE REMEMBER BRIAN. AS WE STARTED THE BEMIDJI EARLY BIRD CROSS COUNTRY MEET THE DAY AFTER BRIAN'S DEATH, WE DIDN'T HAVE A MOMENT OF SILENCE- WE GAVE A YELL TO THE SKIES IN TRIBUTE TO A SPECIAL MAN. IN SPITE OF ALL THAT LIFE HAD THROWN HIS WAY, HE STILL LIVED AND TOUCHED OUR LIVES IN A VERY SPECIAL WAY.

The day the marathon that will be described in the Mile 26 of this book takes place there will be another race. It will be the 10th Annual "BK5K" that is held in Brian's memory. Minneapolis people will have the annual run that Brian's running friends, girl friend, and doctor host every year. Many Twin Cities runners will go to that trail that surrounds one of those Minneapolis lakes, and hopefully some of them will experience the same "runner's high" as did Brian.

I ran the inaugural "BK5K" in 1998. Brian's parents were there and walked the course, and about 300 of us had a very nice run. Probably due to the great reasons the race was first started, it continues to do well. It has been established as a great cancer fund raiser but also a high quality five kilometer run. The winner this past spring ran 14:43 for the men and the top lady was 16:57. Brian would be proud of those quality performances and I am very happy his legacy continues. This photo is of the t-shirt that participants received in the 2007 "BK5K".

Lesson learned: Adversity will come and we never know what life will send our way. We need to fight the good fight, enjoy life to the best of our ability, and enjoy each new day as best we can.

STRUGGLES, GRANDMA'S MARATHON IN DULUTH, MINNESOTA

What does it take to actually run a marathon? Is running 26 miles something anyone can do, or does it take something special? Why is finishing a marathon so difficult one day and so easy, or at least obtainable, the next time you try it? How has my friend Karen been able to finish all but one of her twenty-plus marathons? That time she was forced to stop because of a stress fracture.

Have you ever been to northern Minnesota? If you haven't, and it ever fits your schedule, it might be a good thing to do. One of our Minnesota gems is the other world famous race in Duluth, called "Grandma's Marathon". I am sure when it first began the organizers had no idea it would become so successful and so famous. People like Dick Beardsley and Gary Bjorklund certainly helped it to become increasingly popular. Being a race that always is held in June along Lake Superior, it is generally quite cool and if you hit it on the right year, a tail wind may join you for the trek into town. It is a point to point race that begins outside a small town a little further up north called Two Harbors. Most people are bussed up there, and runners begin on a small tar road that runs along the lake. The starting point is an obscure spot that happens to be 26 miles and 385 yards north of Grandma's Saloon and Restaurant. More and more port-a-pots have shown up over the years, but other than such man-made necessities, runners are entirely surrounded by trees on either side of the road as they await the starting commands. As helicopters fly over and people hang out on the road, the race eventually begins. The views of the lake and the north country certainly have a unique appeal as each runner along the way passes along cabins, small towns, hotels, and resorts before descending upon the city of Duluth.

Some have said the race is all down-hill. The topography of the course does go down in elevation from beginning to end, but don't let that fool you! There are plenty of small up-hills and the course is not that easy. It has many rolling hills, and they do take their toll on your mind and your legs. Other than that, it is a very user-friendly course, and many people feel it is one of the best places to run a good time. Over the years many personal records have been set with Russian runners recently having the most success at Grandma's.

My personal question is: why has that particular race been the site of some of my worst performances? Three times I spend the money to enter, drive over, rent a motel room, and toe the starting line just outside of Two Harbors. Each time resulted in results I am not proud of. We all know that marathoning has become increasingly popular in the past thirty years. As Grandma's Marathon has yielded more participants, the crowd has grown right along with it, and fan enthusiasm in Duluth is as good as anywhere. The whole town and the community seem to view it as their own individual holiday.

One of the times that things didn't work out for me, I literally signed up to run the race with about fifteen of my closest friends. It was one of the worst experiences of my running life! That should have been a very positive situation and from an overall healthy point it was what we should be doing. I was pacing early with three or four buddies, and I was continually looking around for other friends and worrying about how everyone else was doing. An effort of twenty-six miles in length can be a challenge, and I think I have learned that, for me personally, I need to use my mental strength to worry only about me and take care of my needs. In a race of that magnitude it doesn't go well if I spend a lot of time and effort worrying about others. After about sixteen miles I was so shot and so out of it, I just drifted toward the back of the pack and stopped running. I wandered into one of the campgrounds on the west side of the course away from the lake, and stumbled upon a couple. Of course they were complete strangers, and even though I had no idea who they were, I walked right up to them. They were in the process of taking down their tent and breaking camp. I simply asked if they were heading toward Duluth, and they offered me a ride. They also offered me a beer, which I looked at as the happiest thing that had happened to me so far that day. I sat down on a tree stump and waited for them to pack up. It wasn't that hot out, many of my friends did just fine, and I enjoyed the after party in the Duluth Harbor area, just accepting that it was not my day.

The next time I entered Grandma's, the day was a bit warmer and I was in a little better condition to run 26 miles. Things went well for about eight miles. Then, all of a sudden I felt just terrible. It was way too early to begin having problems, and once again I was facing a very long day. Eighteen miles of pain is not something any runner looks forward to, but remember, I can be very stubborn and very determined. I made a continual, slow progression along the course and very consciously decided that this time I would get to the finish line. My pace continued to slow and I interspersed several walking breaks with my jog towards the finish line. After more than an hour of a definite struggle I was over Lemon Drop Hill, at about mile twenty-one, and was approaching the downtown portion of the race. I was being passed by many people, but I was actually doing better than a few other racers. The heat had increased and the mid seventies were not treating some of us too well. I was totally shocked to catch up to my teaching and coaching buddy from back home. I knew if I was able to come from behind and join him that he was certainly not having a good day either. Rather than it being a matter of who finished the race first, it became a matter of who was running the ugliest race. We talked about not having a good day, walked, jogged, and stretched together, and my struggle became a little easier.

Numerous people lined the course from there, through the downtown area and on to the finish line. Together we kept our legs moving. We actually stopped and visited with a few folks we knew who had come over to watch the race. We staggered down the last hill, down around their community center, passed the huge, docked museum boat and through the elaborate finish line area. Finally, the two of us crossed the finish line together. Somehow the ecstatic workers and fans were a whole lot more excited than we were. We had still been able to run the race in three hours and fifteen minutes, but our times were much slower than we had hoped for. However, we had our finishers' medals, and somehow the whole thing still made sense to us. Our training had been at the level where we expected to break three hours, but it just had not been our day to shine. We simply accepted it and headed out of town -or tried to. I met my wife, we started walking towards the car, and I simply proceeded to lie down on the grass on one of the street corners and told her to get the car. She did that for me, and drove down the freeway towards my parent's home while I slept. Some might say what a waste, and the wasted guy just had a good nap. (I had actually finished 940th out of 6,243 runners, but again, expectations had been better than that.)

One other time I had entered the race well ahead of time, which is necessary in order to get in, but had injured myself while training for the race. Once again, it was not to be. I did come up with a theory and decided I needed to address what was going on. As I thought about the dilemma I reached a few conclusions. Even though June in northern Minnesota is generally perfect running weather, something was not working. Being a career school teacher, I realized the race takes place about three weeks after school is out and that was one thing causing me to not be properly focused on running well for 26 miles. I apply myself effectively at being a quality teacher, and the month of May can be very stressful. There are many year end aspects of the job that demand a lot of extra time. As I put myself through the stress of finishing the year, I think my mind is more ready to let down than it is to psych up for something as intense as a marathon. I was also the head track coach for our high school, and about a week after school was out, we were almost always fortunate enough to take various numbers of athletes to the Minnesota State Track and Field Meet. Once again, this is the culmination of months, and sometimes years, of working together with our athletes. Coaches are intent on helping them to do the best they can on the final performance of their season. This is great fun and provides for many great experiences, but it also takes something out of the coaches. The drive to the state meet is about four and a half hours, we spend three days in the Twin Cities, and then the whole school year is over. This is usually one or two weeks before the marathon.

Maybe this is just a rationalization and maybe there is some truth to it, but every Grandma's attempt has brought about questionable results for me. I did wonder if I should even bother to try again and whether or not it would be possible to find success at Grandma's Marathon. During those same Grandma's Marathon years, I had joined teams to run the Edmund Fitzgerald eight-person relay in the fall of the year. This event is also held north of Duluth, and I had posted some phenomenal times. The course is further up the coast of Lake Superior, but it is near the same area with the same kind of racing conditions. Actually, the two twenty-kilometer legs that start the race are probably more hilly than any part of the marathon course. I had been the beginning runner twice and had done the second leg once, running well every time. As a matter of fact, in 1991 I ran a 1:22:09 for the 20k, averaging a quality 6:37 per mile. Granted that was October, and I've always felt more comfortable with cooler conditions, but the Grandma's dilemma was still there.

About this time they started including a half marathon along with the full 26 miler. Some years I opted to run that, probably a more ideal distance for me. Half marathons and ten milers have always felt like they fit my abilities. Some years we just traveled to Duluth and watched friends and others race, always enjoying the numerous festivities that surround the races. Some years I just stayed home and read about the annual trek down Minnesota's north shore and wondered why it never worked out for me.

There are many questions about birth, life and death that are never answered. We never quite know how any one of them are going to work out. The passing away of one of my most treasured mentors would motivate me to attempt to go back to Duluth- one more time .

Lesson learned: Life does not always make sense. One thing that may be questionable is running the marathon. Looking back, I am still happy I experienced each and every trip, and I did gain insight, knowledge, and fellowship even though my finish times didn't please me. Some days things just don't work out.

13

GRANDMA'S MARATHON SUCCESS, 1993
AT 40 YEARS OF AGE!

"Hey, you're here already; how did your race go?"

"Nothing to complain about; it really felt good."

"Well, what was your time? You look okay."

"2:54, and I'm really happy...." My speech trailed away because when my young stud college running friend heard my time, he was so embarrassed that he turned and walked away. But all that is the ending, and I guess I should start at the beginning.

As I have mentioned, historically Grandma's had been a disaster in the making for me. I had made honest efforts three times, and I had felt all three were miserable attempts and minor accomplishments. I did find the finish line that one time, but it wasn't pretty. I do believe that some people were not meant to run marathons, and I do believe that on some days, things just do not work for my body to run 26 miles.

In the fall of 1992 a very important person in my life died while running. Tom Rowlette was a newly-retired teacher who had finished Grandma's Marathon several times. He would always buy one of their awesome artist's renditions of the race, and have it mounted in our local middle school where he was a physical education teacher. He had been a football coach and had carried several extra pounds in his younger years, but became a born-again runner in his late forties. He was truly an inspiration to me and many others in our community. His enthusiasm and excitement for running had become one of the most important aspects of his life. He was the most instrumental person in our area to begin a rather loosely organized running group named, "The North Country Pounders". You won't see our name in many record books. We bought a few racing uniforms together, we entered many local races, and some years we entered teams in the Edmund Fitzgerald Relay. Our group gathered every Saturday morning for runs of various distances and breakfast for those who wanted to get together. I was never sure if the "pounders" had to do with pounding the pavement with our feet while we were running or pounding our favorite beers after a race, but either reason will suffice.

One typical Saturday morning, the local runners gathered to do our thing, and about eighteen of us took off running along Lake Bemidji to the north on our favorite road. Some went out hard to cover a longer distance, and some went easier just to do a Saturday morning jog together. It was one of those early fall days and several rummage sales were taking place all along the residential route. Tom and a friend, being some of the older members of the group, were taking it really easy and stopping at the sales that looked interesting. I am sure neither really needed much, nor were they serious about shopping, but nevertheless they were checking them out. At one of the homes, Tom said he would just stay outside and stretch while our friend went in to check out the bargains. When he came back he found Tom collapsed by the steps! After a couple of easy miles, which should normally have been nothing to Tom, he had a massive heart attack and passed away. It was sad that he perished so soon after he had retired, but somehow it may have made sense that he died while out running with his favorite people and on his favorite road.

Having established our home over three hours away from any close family members, I sometimes reached out to people for special connections. Tom was one of those people. He had become a bit of father figure for me and we had a mutual respect for each other. I think he was quite impressed with the quality of my running, and I always loved his dedication and his attitude. He usually had something witty to say, was glad to share life on the run with anyone, and always had a smile to share. That September day while gathered around his gravesite, I knew something had to be different because Tom was no longer with us. I decided I would run Grandma's Marathon the following June in his honor.

I am sure my new motivation helped me train throughout that entire school year. Being the local cross country and track coach I usually found time during those seasons to do some quality running. For the winter months, I had found a deal for a membership at the local college which has all the newest machines, weight room, and a nice indoor 200 meter track. It was there that I spent some time with the college kids and even did some training with them. Not that I could keep up with them or push them on their quality stuff, but I was honestly able to follow somewhat close to them on workouts requiring more endurance. I also joined them on some outdoor distance work, and the combination seemed to work well. Two of the guys in particular ran the longer distances, and we formed one of those runner bonds that only show up through sweating and working to exhaustion. I was pleased they would allow a thirty-nine-year-old "has been" to follow them around the track, and they allowed me to share a few strategies with them about how they could compete at a higher level.

My training had the consistent balance of speed work with the college runners and increased levels of weekly mileage. I gradually built up to where I ran more the sixty miles the third and fourth weeks prior to the race. My desire to run well had been building for nine months and my motivational problems of the past had been analyzed and understood. I really hoped I was ready to drive back to Duluth and run well at Grandma's Marathon. The nine month approach to the race had gone well. My monthly mileage from January to May was 106 miles, 125 miles, 137 miles, 178 miles in April, and 187 for the month of May.

Previous downfalls for me at Grandma's Marathon in Duluth had to do with running with others and the time of the year. Why did I feel this time things could be different? I was still teaching full-time and still the head track coach; however, I now had the motivation of running the race for my friend Tom, in addition to a full nine months of preparation. It was my goal to follow that usual hectic spring schedule with a marathon that I would be proud of. It takes some special consideration, older age wisdom, or just a lot of luck to run well. I knew of a few others who would be entering the race again, but I didn't train with them very much, and I had no plans of running the race with them. I guess that was a selfish decision, but I had made my plan and I was determined to see it through.

Mentally, I was working on myself to accept that Northern Minnesota in June should be a great place and time to run. The areas of Duluth and Lake Superior are a beautiful, natural setting. Putting those factors together with a great sponsor, an enthusiastic and dedicated race director like Scott Keenan, and throw in some rich tradition, and it should result in a great formula for success. All those good things, and I had succumbed to failure three times. I knew it was really just a mental block and believed I could get past it. I have read every Runner's World magazine and many other books and articles on running, and I knew I needed to get my thinking straight. I did a lot of mental as well as physical preparation, and I began to use a mantra to remind me not to let my mind block my progress towards the finish line. I am not sure if I read it, adopted it, or made it up, but my personal mantra became, "THERE IS NO WALL."

June 19th, 1993, I was forty years old and back in that starting area of Grandma's marathon one more time. If you have not yet been to that particular race start, we are not talking big city starting line. We are talking awesome race start atmosphere- but again there were ghosts that I needed to forget about. I needed to acknowledge the woods, the trees, the sunshine, and the road that would lead the field once again to downtown Duluth. There were some nice clear skies to start the day, and as we started racing down the winding, hilly small country road I began to drill myself on my pace. My goal number for the day was, once again, seven minutes per mile. I would hear or see my mile time, do the math, and determine my specific time goal for the next mile. This was working well. I proceeded to click away the miles, always coming close to the seven minute per mile average. If there was a little extra downhill or uphill, my times reflected that, but I was processing everything in a positive way and it was making sense. As we progressed beyond ten miles, the skies began to change. Very often the early morning sky conditions become the exact opposite as the day actually begins to unfold. Clouds started to form above our heads.

The whole time I felt like I was holding back just a little. I knew I had more to give of myself, and I had the ability to run even faster. I forced myself to accept these as being positive attributes, and I stayed within myself and kept my consistent pace. I stayed strong and passed quite a few people. At mile seventeen and a half it began to sprinkle. I heard my time at mile eighteen and decided to begin to let my pace go a little faster. The plan had been to hold back until the twenty mile mark, but it was very apparent the heat was not going to be a problem. I was feeling like eight more miles would be very obtainable on this particular day. I began a mild assault on the finish line, thinking I would attack until Lemon Drop hill at mile twenty-one, then proceed to cruise into downtown with a smooth, aggressive stride. I was able to get on pace and gradually my splits began to break the seven minute per mile time by ten and even fifteen seconds. I was confidently striding through downtown, hearing the people and feeling they were there to help me this time, rather that thinking they were feeling sorry for me. I made it through downtown, made my left turn off main street, and felt ready to do the

downhill hard that would lead me to the DECC community center. I continued to pass several others who appeared to be struggling, and I made it around the DECC, and past the huge, retired, red and white docked ship. I felt great going into my second to the last right turn. I continued to work hard as I ran two more blocks into the last right turn, and then really was energized by the crowd noise as I headed into that awesome finish area. I made it to the snow fence, the bleachers, and focused on the clock over the street. This finish structure, on that day, seemed to have been made for me. My name and home-town were announced and I finished the Grandma's Marathon in grand style!

I proudly received my finisher's medal, but I needed help to remove my timing chip, and I staggered to a bench off to my right and I carefully sat down. At that point I began to cry. Tom had been with me for the past nine months, Tom was with me today, and I was so very happy to have finished a good race in his honor. I needed to, in my own way, pay tribute to him. A medical person came over to check on me. He asked me if I was doing okay. I told him I was absolutely fantastic and thanked him for asking. I had run the marathon at forty years of age in 2 hours and 54 minutes, the same time I had as a young college team member back in 1971. It was one of the happiest experiences as a runner that I have ever had. After getting a grip on things, I headed into the food area to replenish myself with some post-race refreshments. It was then that I met up with the college stud that I had spent many hours with the previous winter. I had beaten him by about one minute, obviously having passed him in the last portion of the race but never noticing him. He said his other

team mate was even further behind and when he heard my time he couldn't even talk to me. My mistakes, my experiences, had served me well and I had found success in Duluth, Minnesota. I had finished 212th out of 4.272 runners that day. I had finally conquered the Grandma's Marathon course! Okay, maybe I didn't look that great, but looks can be deceiving.

(Both running photos provided by, and used with permission, of Marathon Foto.)

GRANDMA'S MARATHON
June 19, 1993
Marathon Foto

In retrospect, my fortieth year of life was actually quite a running year for me all the way around. I don't know if it was my way of dealing with turning forty or if everything just fell into place, but check out these numbers. I had finished second overall in the spring 10k in Bemidji, finishing ahead of two very accomplished competitors, and had run a 36:56. Later that summer, I finished a half marathon in 1:25 and also did a masters'

15k in 59 minutes. For whatever reasons, it had been a very good racing season for me. Maybe it did make sense that it was my best Grandma's ever. Maybe I just wanted Tom to be proud of my running and of me...

Lesson learned: Dedication, long range planning, and motivation can have a huge effect on the results of a marathon.

13.1

MENTAL RAMBLINGS HALF WAY THROUGH A RACE

There are many reasons why I run. One of those is the mental wanderings that my mind goes through on sort of a sub-conscious level. Problems and situations just seem to pop into my mind and I sometimes work on them, sometimes decide they aren't that important, and very often make a plan as to what to do with them. This chapter on random thoughts reflects how I see things in the middle of a distance run. I am out there enjoying the miles and just drifting along as many different kinds of thoughts seem to surface. I would like to share a few of those random thoughts as I am now half way through the writing of this book.

ALL TIME WORSTS AND BESTS

FAVORITE RACE EVER: Las Vegas Half Marathon: It was literally down hill… then flat… a beautiful morning, wind at the back, perfect temperature… a great race atmosphere with the course beginning out in the country and ending on the edge of the strip. It used to be held on the fourth weekend in January.

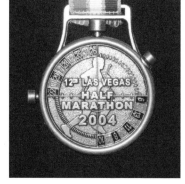

BEST POST RACE: Tears of joy after finishing Grandma's Marathon with a 2:54 effort… I had trained for nine months, finished ahead of two college kids I knew, and just felt great. Medical people thought I was crying in pain, and I told them everything was wonderful!

BEST DROP OUT EXPERIENCE: Seventeen miles of a Wisconsin marathon, I dove into a lake and had the greatest swim ever. It made so much of the hurt just melt away.

BEST RACE/WORST REPERCUSSION: Sixty-two minute ten miler in a thin racing flat... not very smart...things didn't work out so well. This race started a long period with plantar fasciitis.

DOCTOR'S NEWS IN MY 30'S: "Sure we can use cortisone, but you still need to be careful." (It didn't really help my plantar fasciitis and it bothered me for months.)

SHOE THAT LEAD TO HEATHY FEET: Saucony Jazz 5000- I don't know if it was the timing or the shoe, but my foot finally felt fine... bought two more pairs of them.

DOCTOR'S NEWS IN MY 40'S: "The way this hamstring looks, it is maybe time to stop doing intervals with the teenagers." (It would always continue to be sensitive, and I would need to train carefully to keep things working correctly.)

DOCTOR'S NEWS IN MY 50'S: "No, you can't eat whatever you want just because you are a runner."

FAVORITE INDOOR CROSS TRAINING: Elliptical machine. I really like this machine! It works well for endurance workouts as well as intervals and it has been much easier on my hamstrings, hips, and knees.

FAVORITE OUTDOOR CROSS TRAINING: Cross country skiing,.. a great alternative to help enjoy Minnesota winters. We don't always get adequate snow, but most years it works out for a couple of months. The classical technique allows me to really enjoy the rhythmic, smooth glide across the snow.

BEST CLOTHING ADAPTATION: Half tights... I have worn them all the time for the last twenty years. All equipment stays in place. All inner thigh chafing is eliminated.

MOST APPRECIATED APPAREL: Wind brief. Some things were just meant to stay warm! In case you have never heard of such a thing, they are extra warm underwear with a special windproof layer of material across the front.

SMARTEST PURCHASE EVER: Gortex running suit. Along with polypropylene clothing worn underneath, it makes almost any weather manageable. When you live and run in negative twenty-five degrees, that becomes important.

SHOE THAT I'VE PURCHASED THE MOST: Nike Air Pegasus.

SHOE THAT I APPRECIATE THE MOST NOW KNOWING ALL PERSONAL BEST TIMES ARE BEHIND ME: Nike Air Shox: I hope they keep making them...I love the cushioning.

CRAZIEST COACHING BREAKTHROUGH: Our 1996 girls 4 X 800 team ran faster than their ever optimistic, positive coach thought they could. Broke our school record and collected third place medals from the Minnesota State Meet.

MOST SURPRISING STOPWATCH TIME: In 1997 my boys 4 x 800 relay team, in a regular season meet, ran a 7:58.4. That was indeed a great day!

MOST AWESOME RECRUITING CALL: The University of Minnesota running coach called, "We want two of your athletes to join the Minnesota Gophers."

BEST HIGH SCHOOL PERFORMANCE: Brian Kraft winning the 1981 Minnesota State Track Meet in both the mile and the two mile. His best times for his senior year were 4:15.9 for 1600 meters and 9:13.7 for 3200 meters.

BEST COLLEGIATE PERFORMANCE BY A FORMER BHS ATHLETE: Luke Mullranin, A University of Minnesota competitor, surpassing his previous third place finish in the Big 10 Steeple Chase by finishing second in 2004. (He was also named most valuable Cross Country runner his senior year after leading the Gophers at Nationals.)

BEST PERSONAL RACE I WITNESSED BY A FORMER ATHLETE: I was able to watch Luke Mullranin race to second at the Big 10 meet. He always ran from behind. As early as fourth grade in my Physical Education class, he would start far back and gradually work his way up to the front. He ran all through high school and college using the same very effective racing tactic. His training, often running the six miles from his house to school or back home, was always consistent. He always believed he could do big things...and he did.

BEST SHOT AT OLYMPIC TRIALS BY A BEMIDJI ATHLETE: In 2004, Luke was within ten people of making the trials' qualification. In the same year, Rebekah Walter missed an invitation to the Olympic Trials in the Steeple by one person.

BEST ROAD RACE BY MY ATHLETES: Pete Miller was the top Minnesotan at Twin Cities Marathons and ran a 2:28.

SILLIEST COACHING TECHNIQUE: Running alongside Stacey Mills, who once held our 800 meter record, with my flat hand over her head. We needed to solve her bouncing problem, and solve it we did as she earned a college scholarship to Jamestown College in North Dakota and eventually to Adam's State in Colorado. She became a NCAA Division II Cross Country Champion and still runs today.

BEST COACHING COMMAND TO YELL: "Cookies!" I used to remind my 4:15 miler to straighten out his right arm swing.

LARGEST TRACK TEAM COACHED: 107 Girls!

LARGEST CROSS COUNTY TEAM COACHED: 58 Runners!

BIGGEST SURPRISE WHILE COACHING GIRLS: My 1996 girls 4 X 800 relay team was in the state meet and ran a very close race. Three seniors ran the first legs and a freshman anchored the race and had an awesome finish. The race was very close from third to seventh, and we had no idea where we had finished. The announcer called the 7th team, not us… the 6th, then the 5th, then the 4th, and finally we were called up for the 3rd place medals… and we were ecstatic!

BIGGEST SURPRISE WHILE COACHING BOYS: Jesse Prince, team mate of Luke, competed in the 1999 Minnesota State Track Meet, following the expected mile winner and #1 runner in the state and staying close to him. Jesse placed second in the state, running a 4:17 mile, our second fastest time in the history of our school.

GREATEST HONOR EVER RECEIVED: I have been named both Girl's Minnesota State Cross Country Coach of the Year and Boy's Minnesota State Cross Country Coach of the Year. The award for my boys was the bigger honor because we were rated fourth in the state. Two of my top five didn't make it to the finish line at state, and we still finished ninth…and they still elected me Coach of the Year.

MOST STRESSFUL PERFORMANCE: During a very, very strong wind for the last ten miles of a thirteen and a half mile road race, a friend and I took turns each mile blocking the wind on the side for each other.

MOST SURPRISING FINISH: 3:07 at Kansas City Marathon after only five weeks of intentional training.

GREATEST RUNNING GIFT: A shoe dryer from my sister-in-law and her husband. (If you don't have one, a great trick I've used is to stuff wet running shoes with newspaper, so they dry faster and keep their toe box shape.) This dryer has two tubes that stick up and a last-shaped piece at the top. Place your shoes upside down on it and very slowly it blows warm air through the shoes to dry them out.

NEWEST TECHNOLOGICAL APPRECIATION: Moisture repellent shirts. Feels great and works well for indoor gym workouts and hot summer days.

GREATEST SUPER HERO EXPERIENCE: Beating Spiderman! Imagine my surprise when I was in mile four of a half marathon, and I caught up to Spiderman. Never having raced a superhero before, I followed him to the turn around point, and as we headed toward the finish with the wind on our backs, I made a "super" move, leaving him behind.

BEST POST-RUN FEELING: JUMPING IN THE MISSISSIPPI IN MY BACKYARD AFTER A SUMMER WORKOUT. How lucky we are to live on the river… twenty-five feet across and normally about four feet deep. After a workout the clean, refreshing water really helps to cool down the body.

CRAZIEST WORKOUT EVER PLANNED: A college buddy and I planned to run from Bemidji to Park Rapids, 50 miles away. He came down with mono while we were training for it, and I can proudly say I have never run further than 26 miles! Maybe some crazy day in my life that will change… but I doubt it…

CRAZIEST WORKOUT I HAVE PLANNED FOR THE VERY NEAR FUTURE: Run 24 miles in 24 hours, 1 mile for each and every hour for 24 in a row. My headlamp will help… I'm just waiting for the first warm spring evening…

MOST APPRECIATED MODERN TECHNOLOGICAL CREAM: Body Glide. Solves all my blister problems that have haunted me for many years…or maybe it's the blister preventative sock, I am not sure…

MOST BEAUTIFUL RUN: North of San Francisco near our rented beach house. My daughter and I headed out for an early morning run. Waves landed quietly, but with a rhythm and a sound all their own. Gulls flew around checking for breakfast being washed on-to the shore. We made two beautiful paths of footprints in the flat, wet sand.

14

EELPOUT PEEL-OUT, WALKER, MINNESOTA, 2006

It was February in northern Minnesota, and the crazy town of Walker was hosting a wild event called the "Eelpout Peel-out"! An eelpout is an ugly rough fish that I don't think anyone would ever really enjoy catching except on this particular weekend. The Walker peel-out is a five-mile race in the winter that starts with a huge downhill towards Leech Lake and then follows a basic figure eight course south of town into the country and finishes back at the local High School.

There were eighty-nine runners competing in 2006, and it was sixteen degrees at race start. I know many folks cannot even fathom the idea of running on snowy, icy roads at that temperature, but believe it or not, it was a rather mild day for this race. My basic running clothes have always been either blue or black for winter running, and I chose black for this particular day. As I drove the thirty-five miles down from Bemidji, there were a few slippery, icy spots and I remember hoping my racing flats would be adequate for traction for the day, but I did have two other pairs of shoes just in case. I wore one pair of blister-preventing socks, Nike racing flats, half-tights, heavy wind-resistant polypro full running tights, black shorts, the same heavy polypro running top, an additional black long-sleeved racing top, black semi-thick gloves, a black balaclava and a baseball cap over the top of the balaclava. In case you have only seen a balaclava in the magazines, it completely covers your head, and neck with various-sized openings for your eyes, nose and mouth. I used a very thin one for this day, and had my mouth covered earlier in the race but it was exposed most of the way. Yes, all this extra clothing does slow one down, but it is important not to freeze anything that is important to you and yours. For colder running, I have a thicker balaclava, but also wind briefs, a Gore-Tex suit, and heavier gloves, mittens, and hats. None of which seemed needed for the day.

The race commands were rather relaxed. On your mark. Get set, and then we were all told to yell, "POUT!"--- So we did, and the race was off. I had checked out the competitors for the day whom I knew, and took a relaxed start in eighth position. I was following the new "upstart" gentleman from my hometown whose kids have reached the age where he is now training very hard, and for the past year or so, he has become a lot faster. I really didn't like how slow he was starting, so I moved ahead of him as we were running down a long five block hill. Small town events are always busy and fun and sure enough, they had the Minnesota State Highway that runs through the town blocked off to traffic. We took a right on that highway, ran right down the center of town and out into the country on about eight blocks of main street/ highway. My new rival had passed me a ways back, and then a quality runner I knew from Canada came cruising by just as I was settling into a nice pace in ninth position. My baseball cap had already come off, (oops, misjudged the temperature), so I shoved that down the front of my shorts, and took off my gloves and held them instead of wearing them. Sometimes one needs to make decisions even while the race is going on. A tall, younger man pulled up next to me at about a mile and half and I finally sensed my pace was about right. I had established where I belonged in the field of runners for that day. We stayed together for a while, coming through two miles in 13:36. This next part was on a loop road by Leech Lake and angled around to the left and through a snowy ditch trail that my shoes and my nerves did not enjoy. Next we went straight across the highway and out onto a loop, veering the other way to form the bottom circle of the figure eight. Another younger, shorter person pulled up next to us, and I decided not to just let him go on by. He seemed determined and had come up fast, but I had reached the point where I just didn't want anyone else to go by me. We finished the far loop and came back to the highway for a left turn that would take us back in to town. He asked if we cut through the snowy ditch again like we had before or if we stayed on the road. I said it would be the road, and at that moment decided to use the aggressive approach on the turn to go ahead of him. About twenty yards past the turn someone, dressed in very colorful clothing whom I had not seen before, came cruising up and passed right on by. This was at about three and one-half miles, and I was not happy that someone else was now in the picture. Facing a long gradual up hill, I had the new colorful guy and the two younger fellows all around me. The new racer insisted on running either to the right of the side rumble strips that warn cars if they are going off the road or way to the left of them. I felt it was too slippery off to the left so I either drafted on him when he was on the edge of the main road or kept pace along side of him when he moved further off onto the shoulder.

After fifteen seconds of jockeying for position, even though it was a half mile long uphill, I decided to surge to the top and put some distance on the three guys that were bothering me. My wife and I had been spending some time that winter at a local indoor training facility and I had been doing a lot of training on the elliptical machine with arm pulls. Feeling strong and hitting the hill hard, I was able to put some distance on all of them and get out there by myself. It always feels good to be able to make a strong move like that late in a race. Within a half-mile of the finish, we made a left turn onto a road with the worst conditions of the entire race. The road wound around some buildings, making three or four short quick turns, and it included three small uphill stretches. All of the inclines were snow and ice covered and at the point where, of course, we were the most tired. To my surprise, the second young guy who had caught up to me surged ahead at the very end with a twenty year old kick that I had thirty years ago. I didn't even respond and I finished in tenth place overall with a good run on a winter morning. My time was 34:26 which I found very pleasing, and it made me really happy that I could average well under seven minutes a mile in those conditions. After getting the second place ribbon for the 50-59 age group (what my wife calls the *old fart division*) and my Canadian friend received first place, we headed down to a local restaurant. Six of us relaxed with a little pizza, a celebratory beer, and some great socializing. Maybe some would frown on that after some hard exercise, but we sure had a good time.

Lesson learned: Quick finishes get more difficult as we age, but they probably don't make that much difference.

15

O O

CHILDREN AND A FAMILY HALF MARATHON

A CHILD, A RUNNER, A LEADER

Cross Country Camp When You are Only 6
Can Cause a Guy to Put up a Fuss.
"Daddy, Daddy can I Please go With?"
*That 20 Inch Bike **Would** Keep up With Us*

He Wanted to Play Pool, He Wanted to Swim
He sat Around the Campfire, Just Havin' Fun
He Learned, He Helped Dad With Stuff
He Saw it All, and Yes, He Began to Run!

Legs Grew Longer, He Did a Race or Two
Got His Picture in the Paper, Won a Ribbon Too
He Wore the T-shirts, Didn't Like to Lose
Joined the Middle School Team and Really Began to Cruise

Legs Grew Longer, and High School Began
He Joined Dad's Team, and Away He Ran
Made Varsity as a Sophomore, and Ran With Pride
Made Many Friends, and Enjoyed the Ride

Legs Grew Longer, and Captain He Became
Other Coaches Knew Him, and Called Him by Name
The Team Stretched, They Jogged, They Raced, They Listened
A Leader by Example, A Man on a Mission

After 15 Years at CC Camp, at the Skill Crane he was Great
He Led the Team Well, and no, They Never Made it to State
But He Smiled, He Ran, He did his Best
He Made Things go Well; He Helped Lead the Rest

Being 6 Feet Tall and 4 Inches More
With Bouncing Red Hair, He was Hard to Ignore
Watching Him, Timing Him, Along Every Step of the Way
It is Easy to be Proud and Have Good Things to Say

A Child. A Runner, A Leader, Our Son
Thanks for Being Here. I Would Say, WE WON!

The greatest gift I ever received was the honor of becoming a father. My life has been good, many things have worked well, but being a parent and a dad has been the best. I do, and would love our kids no matter what, but the athletic and fitness lifestyle has been an important part of their lives. The coolest aspect of all was that we were given this gift three times.

By the time I accomplish Mile 26 of this book, all three of our children will be college graduates. They have all graduated from high school with honors, and they all received scholarships to colleges. They have all been very different, but in so many ways they have been the same. They have all been involved in music but attended three very different colleges. Once again we have been blessed, and I truly believe they were all led to the right college for them. Each began college the first fall after high school graduation, remained at the same college they originally decided to attend, and all three graduated with honors in four years.

Our oldest, Matthew Dennis Bartz Matt Handsome Charlie Brown, or just plain Matt, is not, was not, and probably never will be a runner. When he was in the community youth track meets as a three-year-old, he was so far behind in a 200 meter race, he actually thought he was winning. Yes, we started them early. When he was about twelve-years-old, I remember he had spent a day traveling with the local club swim team. That evening at home, he stood on the landing of our bedroom level, and the two of us were discussing our day. He threw his foot up on the railing and continued to stretch out first one leg and then the other, as we visited. I have no recollection as to how his races had gone that day, but I knew he was destined to continue with his swimming career. It had become something that he valued, that mattered to him, and it had become an important part of his life. I have never forgotten that moment because it triggered great pride in who our son was for many years to come. I knew he had discovered the joy, the responsibility, the value of being an athlete.

Matt would continue with his club swimming, add a high school swimming career, and eventually become a varsity swimmer at Hamline University in St. Paul, Minnesota. Athletics and swimming became the stability factor for his four years of college. While being primarily a breast stroker in high school, college found him gravitating toward distance freestyle events. There was never a reason he should become a distance runner, but it sure seemed familiar when he became a distance swimmer and his specialty became, what else, swimming the mile. We were very proud of his hard work and effort, and thankful his coach and fellow swimmers were such a supportive group to encourage his healthy lifestyle throughout his four years of college. He was given the opportunity to lead others as captain of his college swim team during his senior year.

Traci just seemed like she was always a natural endurance athlete. I don't remember any kind of question as to whether or not she would be in track, cross country skiing, and cross country running. She was an important part of those sports all during middle school and high school. My earliest and clearest recollection of her racing in a cross country meet was a race during her middle school years. She had a different coach at that level, but we competed on the same schedule. The race was progressing well, and I was out on the golf course positioned a little past the half way mark. I stood on a rise off to the east and encouraged, well okay, yelled, as the runners came by. While really making my thoughts known to my daughter she abruptly replied, "Shut up, Dad!" I knew that I needed to re-evaluate my methods of encouragement. I must have been quite successful at that because she would go on to be a very important runner in both of our programs and she eventually lead all three of her sports as captain her senior year. She was part of one of the fastest 4 X 800 teams in Minnesota her senior year. One of my toughest moments as a runner's dad and a coach was watching Traci's team miss qualifying for the Minnesota State Cross Country Meet by one lousy point.

College for Traci found her at one of the best Division III schools in the nation. As parents, we thought she was headed there to be part of the Cross Country Skiing Team; however, it seemed that from day one she became a complete runner for their program. At St. Olaf College virtually the entire track team is also involved in their Cross Country Running Team. They are a very close knit group and Traci fit in immediately. I will never forget the first time I saw 65 college coeds, hanging around before the race in loose, unmatched sweats. As they finished their warm-up and it came time to line up at the starting line, they headed to team camp for last minute preparations. When the entire team came to the starting line, they had shed the unmatched sweats and proudly wore black leotard racing uniforms with the bold, gold St. Olaf written across the chest. They were ready to run. Unfortunately, we didn't see them win every time, but they were always very competitive. We did see them win the MIAC Conference Championships every year, but we were especially proud when they kept the streak alive and won it during

Traci's senior year when she served the program as one of the team captains.

Being Traci's only running coach prior to college, I could relate to her continual career and tried to be a part of her races when I could. I was still the local high school coach of both of her sports, so it wasn't always easy to get to her college races. Her college campus was about four and a half hours away from our home. One fall I did drive down alone to see one of her meets, and I saw a great race. There were about eight schools participating on a very muddy, rainy, warm day, and the Ole's had once again done well. After the meet a couple of groups of girls asked the coach if they could run and dive into the standing water on the course. She informed them that they could, but to be careful and not to wear their uniforms in the mud. I wasn't aware of all that, and Traci asked me to jog out with her on the cool down after the race. I jogged with her for about a half mile on the course and saw more than twenty college girls in their various brands and styles of underwear, playing in the water and the mud. It was hilarious, and a bit embarrassing as the father of one of the best mudders. It was even more embarrassing when I became the designated photographer to help them remember the day, but it was really good "clean" fun and the team togetherness and happiness were apparent.

Once again I felt one of my children was at the perfect college to meet her needs. Traci valued and cherished many things about St. Olaf Cross Country, Track, and her academic as well as her social life. She graduated with honors in 2003, after four years of studies, and with a double major. She obtained a degree in Mathematics, as well as a degree, with distinction, in Biology.

Jacob, although never a college athlete, was probably our most athletic child. He was determined and showed promise from a very young age. My earliest memory of Jacob's athletic prowess was when he was about six years old, and he and I entered a race in our local state park. There was a small loop four kilometer race and a larger eight kilometer race. The plan was for me to do the longer run and Jake the smaller, and we would probably get done at approximately the same time. Mom was along to keep an eye on us, and off we went on the trail. When the 4k was just about over, instead of going straight and to the finish of the race, Jake turned left and headed out on the 8k part of the course. That last portion was lariat-style where you run a portion, do a circle, and come back on the same trail. I was somewhere among the top five runners, and as we came back on the very last portion of the race, I shockingly met little Jake going out on the wrong course. What was a dad to do? Well, he was with a lady I knew quite well, and she told me not to worry; he would be fine. I finished through the chute alongside beautiful Lake Bemidji, quickly did a U-turn, and headed back out on the course. By the time I reached him he was finishing the loop part and crying quite hard. I gave him a hug, we talked, and he still wanted to finish. And he did. At six years of age Jake completed a race of almost five miles in length. Afterwards he was a little sore, but it probably helped a little bit that he was the proud winner of the youngest age group.

Jake would continue on to be involved in basketball, track, and he would find his most success in cross country running. Just like Traci, he ran all seven years of middle school and high school cross country. He was a great captain and competed very well as a high school runner.

College would find him facing a busy schedule with a music/business major and his time would be spent on those efforts. He considered joining the college running teams and watched former people he competed against do quite well, but he had clear goals in mind as to what he wanted to accomplish. Dedicated time with a college athletic team didn't fit that schedule.

Jake and I seem to have the ability to go out and run whenever we want to do it. He has run half marathons with as little training as going out for a jog on three different workouts. My abilities are similar in that I could not run a step for two or three months and be able to go out for a five or six mile run whenever I felt like it. We've been blessed with a lot of natural endurance and have shared runs, races, and triathlons together as father and son.

I am very proud that all three of our children were involved in athletics. They learned discipline, dedication, loyalty, discernment, and appreciation through their running and swimming. Athletics provided so much joy and so many positive experiences for my children that it had much to do with who and what they have become. It seems that an active, healthy lifestyle will continue to be part of their adult lives as well. It feels awesome that as a family we would promote healthy values and that all three children will continue to pursue positive lifestyles in their own individual ways.

During June of 2001 we had a family exercise experience that was one of the best. Three of us decided to enter Grandma's Half Marathon. I was a forty-eight year old has-been that would probably never quit running. Traci was half way through her college career, and Jake was going to be a junior in high school. The starting line was thirteen miles up the coast of Lake Superior in rural, northern Minnesota on a small, tarred, country road. The race has a reputation of having many walkers, and it has a 6:30 am start. They do such a great job of putting on a quality race, the premise being that an early morning start provides ideal temperatures and almost completely clears the finish area for the marathoners to finish their race. We were bussed up and spent our time stretching, using the facilities, and getting prepared. We made our bag drop and started wandering through the crowd toward the starting line. Even though my children have accomplished some great feats, they still are not as assertive as they could be in some situations. I have run this race several times, and while they listened to a certain extent, they were not willing to move up very close to the starting line. Traci stopped quite far back, Jake came up a little further and I stood next to him. I looked at the people around us and knew we were still not up far enough. He was not willing to go up any further, but I maneuvered up another fifteen rows or so. It is always a hard thing to know what to do, but with my long strides I do not enjoy being overly crowded at the beginning of a race.

As the gun was fired and the pack started to move, I was very happy I had moved up. The first half mile was still very crowded and it took at least that long to get my normal stride flowing down the road. We would all be fortunate to have a good run on that early June morning. My dedicated wife couldn't believe how close together we all finished. I did stay in front, mainly due to my starting position, and finished in 1 hour, 36 minutes, and 1 second. Jake was next in 1:39:31, and Traci finished two minutes later at 1:41:44. She was actually in 568th place overall out of 3,787 runners, and she finished fourth in the women's 18, 19 age group.

We watched some of the marathon, the most exciting part being watching a former athlete, Pete Miller, finish in twenty-third place with a fine time of 2:26.08. After some lunch, it was a unanimous vote to return to the motel and take a nap. Waking up at 4:15 in the morning and running a very nice early morning half marathon had left us all exhausted. It had been a wonderful family experience that none of us will ever forget. Experiencing the running effort together strengthened our family bond as runners.

(Photos provided for and used with permission from Marathon Foto)

Lesson learned: A day planned around waking up very early in the morning, preparing for an event together, and going out and sharing the same experience can help to bring a family closer together.

BOSTON #2: WHY?

"When the sidewalk ends, I will probably run on the road.
When the road ends, I will probably run on the trail.
When the trail ends I will probably run on the path.
Where the path divides, I will run the direction that looks most interesting.
When the path end, who knows, I may still keep on running."

Coaching and running many area races have helped me to meet, befriend, admire, and attempt to inspire a lot of people. Sometimes those people are willing to buy you a beer, throw a party, or drive you to the next road race. Sometimes they teach you how to actually get somewhere in the Twin Cities or they share course secrets about an upcoming race. One of those friends, a former high school runner of mine, was actually crazy enough to volunteer to coach with me. This has happened several times, but Dan was very helpful and certainly influenced our team in a positive way. About the third year he helped us out, the fall of 1995, an interesting situation came up after practice one day. He announced he had a room in Boston for the upcoming spring marathon. I was excited and found that interesting, so I asked him where he had qualified. Well, no, that part of the problem he had not taken care of yet.

All too often in life I see a problem, and I just have to find a solution for it. Well, I told Dan we would research the possibilities, find a marathon to run, and make a road trip out of it. He was fine with that, but I didn't really know how my wife would take the news. Surprisingly, she was excited about the idea, so we agreed that the Kansas City Marathon, five weeks away, would be the best for everyone's schedule. I only had one slight problem: I was running about twenty-five miles a week at the time, and I usually prefer to take at least six months to train for a marathon.

How could I get ready in five weeks to run twenty-six miles while I was working full-time and coaching? Now that would take some planning. I sketched it out on a calendar and decided I could do a gradual build up to a sixty mile week which would take me to one week before the trip. Luckily, injuries left me alone, and I was able to find the time I needed to cover those miles. However, it did require a long Sunday afternoon run instead of doing the couch-potato thing for a football game. That sixteen miler was my longest run. During the run a blister developed which forced me to sit down on the side of the road and take off my right sock. Not recommended procedure, but it changed the friction and got me through that run. With a little preventative medicine the spot seemed fine the next day. Those five weeks of recorded mileage in my running log added up 35 miles, 44 miles, 51 miles, and then the 60. I allowed for a mini-taper and did about fourteen miles during the week of the race.

We headed south on a Thursday night after work, drove into the night and found a motel room just inside of Iowa. Continuing on to Kansas City the next day and arrived late in the afternoon- I was impressed with the city and remembered hoping to go back and visit again some day. We checked in at Race Headquarters and found a restaurant to relax and fortify our bodies. I ordered spaghetti with bread and salad, and Dan surprised me by ordering a hamburger and French Fries. I did wonder at the time why he had ordered that, but he was a young adult and a very intelligent guy so I figured it wasn't my place to judge. (Today he is a Physician's Assistant and a successful medical officer in the National Guard.)

The course was unique and downright cool. The start was a long stretch on a medium-sized urban street. It then proceeded to turn left and make its way toward a very upper class housing development. The temperature was somewhat runner-friendly, high forties at the start and topping out in the high fifties. My training seemed to hit things correctly, and I was on my favorite strategy of adding seven minutes to my mile split and hoping to complete the next mile somewhere near that number. We left the affluent area and headed back to the south toward the area we had started from. We were at about eight miles, into the wind, and these two gentlemen would not let me pass them. When I did, they immediately both passed me back. As I got up close, they applied more speed to their pace. I forced myself to grab a steady following pace to analyze what was happening. I knew this back and forth strategy was not the best use of my energy available for good racing. I made a conscious decision to follow them until the next turn. This was almost a mile into the wind, and I simply drafted the entire way. They had frustrated me, but I had made a positive plan as to how to deal with the situation. We came to a turn to the right, and I asserted myself and made a strong move passing the two of them, and this time they did not respond. I never saw them again.

The next section was a very long, steep uphill, about a mile and a half.

After the strong move past the two racers and a positive experience on a long hill, I was feeling good. I kept attacking and moving, with many people coming back to me while I continually kept passing quite a few members of the field. At about mile sixteen I looked ahead and saw a familiar runner. I had passed many other people, but the person most difficult to pass would be my friend Dan. I ran with him for about a half mile; he had hit that wall and things were not going well. I forget the exact problem he was having, but he insisted that I not allow him to slow me down, and I reluctantly left him behind.

The miles and splits kept coming and I knew it was going well. I was feeling strong and continued to keep the pace going toward the finish line. After spending time with Dan and making some calculations, I knew good results were a possibility. I got back to work at following my seven minute plan and began a gradual attack toward the finish line Once I made it across that line, my legs were plenty stiff, and a chair felt really good for a few minutes right after the race. As I was sitting in the chair, I was pleased to see Dan crossing the finish line.

I was happily surprised to be part of the awards ceremony, getting an award for being seventh in the largest age group that ran that day. I had completed the race in 3 hours and 7 minutes. The award was a unique light switch plate made of brushed silver. They actually gave more awards to the age categories that had more people. I appreciated the award, but much bigger than that, I loved the fact that I had qualified for the Boston Marathon!

We had plenty of time to console each other and evaluate our experiences on the long ride home. I will never forget one thing Dan told me while we made that trip back to Minnesota. He let me know that after having been coached by me, after having coached with me, and now after doing a marathon with me, he really had a lot or respect for what I do. I humbly thanked him and told him I was happy and proud we had made the trip. I was also proud that I was able to finish 45th out of 453 marathon finishers.

Not too long after I was back in my home and talking with my wife, I asked the obvious question. Do you want to go to Boston? One thing about my gal: she loves to travel with me. We decided it would be great to go back, having been there in 1979. The coolest part was it was 1995 and that meant I had actually qualified not only to go back to Boston, but for the 100th annual Boston Marathon!

FINISHERS MEDAL FOR THE KANSAS MARATHON

Lesson learned: Training doesn't always have to be completely logical or ideally planned out. Sometimes you can just apply yourself as best you can and still perform very well.

GETTING READY FOR THE 100TH BOSTON

That late October qualifier in Kansas was great, and we followed it up with coaching our teams in the regional and state cross country meets. Then it was time to plan a training schedule that would cover the six months before the Boston Marathon. It was also time to actually register for the race. Things had changed a bit from 1979 to 1996. Believe it or not, the entry fee in '79 was $5.00! Even though we knew and were part of the tremendous changes in the running boom over the past 17 years, we were still shocked to realize the race was going from 8000 to 35000 runners, and the race fee was now eighty dollars.

The date in the log book was January 8, 1996. It reads, "SORE ALL OVER TODAY; YESTERDAY I SKIED TEN MILES IN A RACE." Not a bad accomplishment considering the weather had been so cold it was hard to even make myself get out the door, let alone ski a long distance. We were above the zero mark for the race, but that was the first time in five days. I figured the Boston-bound guys from Texas were not having this same problem. The ski was a nice way to get one and one half hours of aerobic work done on a January day.

The first two weeks of the year yielded eighteen miles each. Not really a planned workout, but it just worked out that way. About half of the work was on the treadmill and about half was outdoors. The week before the ski race, I made it to twenty-two miles and now this ten miles worth of work started out week four on the trail to Boston. Weather sounded good, so I decided to aim for about thirty miles for the next week. My joints were holding up well, and I hadn't frozen anything off yet.

Reflecting back to the fall, I had trained for five weeks and did the Kansas City thing and now it was my fifth week in training for Boston. The effort didn't seem like it was enough for the 100th annual running of the most famous race in America. Tradition, the great city, and the 100th anniversary required a serious effort. One doesn't just fly out, plan for, pay for, and experience Boston without going for it.

That month would end in a very different way than I had anticipated. Our family had always been a close unit and lately our father had been exhibiting some very peculiar behaviors. At the annual family Christmas celebration, he had asked, clearly and distinctly in front of the entire family, if any of the five children would like to have his father's antique tractor. While this may seem like a very normal discussion at a family gathering, the odd thing was that he and I had worked on the tractor the previous summer. He had hired someone to repaint the old Farmall H and it looked great. He had also ordered a full set of original decals to recreate its original look. The two of us spent a very nice Sunday afternoon in August making sure all the decals where properly positioned exactly where they belonged and had mounted them on the tractor together. Afterwards, while having a fresh, cold drink of lemonade with my wife and my mother, he had given me the tractor. I was shocked to be a witness to that Christmas conversation, but in my usual manner of problem solving, I didn't say anything then, intending to work it out later. This was simply not typical of how my father lived his life. Later that week, while my family was still staying with my parents for the holidays, we were playing one of my children's new Christmas games with my parents. It was a word association game, and my dad was making the most abstract, surprising connections and that became very confusing to me. He had always been a very straight forward kind of guy, and this was really not normal.

A few weeks later, my mother called and said dad had been developing more strange behaviors; therefore, they would be getting things checked out. He had actually been trying to read the Bible the previous evening and was unable to make out the words. Subsequent investigation revealed a brain tumor. Toward the end of January we were facing exploratory surgery in Minneapolis.

I wanted to have courage. I needed to remember the great amount of courage he showed me throughout his confrontation with cancer. I'll never forget him walking off to surgery in his hospital gown. With a little hug, and a shrug of his shoulders, he waddles down the hall. He was really never to be the same again. Yes, the cancer was present before that day, but this was the beginning of the end. That January day when we discovered the harsh and cold reality of the situation, Dad faced the diagnosis and all that followed with acceptance and peace. He did it all with courage and dignity, or at least with as much dignity as you can have when day by day you are slowly, constantly, losing more and more of what you have taken for granted your whole life: balance, walking, putting words into sentences, finding the word you want to say, passing food, talking, moving your limbs, using the bathroom, being coherent, and being able to get out of bed. It became a slow, ugly, progression towards non-existence. This overwhelming situation was being experienced while I was planning what now seemed like a frivolous trip to Boston. Training was a welcome relief. It caused me to think deeper and deeper about what life was really all about. I would get in the middle of those long runs and just drift through trying to make sense of everything. I would work the last part of the training run extra hard and just bring myself to welcomed exhaustion. It was decided that my wife and I would still go to Boston, with my parents' blessing. It didn't always feel good, but we made the decision and stuck with it.

The actual surgery was somewhat successful, but the dendrites of the tumor were actually lodged deeper into the gray matter of his brain making it impossible to remove the entire tumor. Dad underwent radiation therapy for thirty-five days straight, excluding weekends, as I continued to train in the months of March and early April. He was even able to see his radiation treatments as a blessing. The treatments took place thirty-five miles away in St. Cloud, Minnesota. He talked about how nice the radiation people were, and how much he enjoyed the fellowship with different friends and relatives who took turns driving my parents over and back. Even though they were daily trips, the folks were able to enjoy many of them. With an attitude like that, how could I not stay positive and focus on making my training as good as it could be?

Because I would be taking some time away from my track team, I came up with a motivational plan that would help me focus and also give me something extra to run for or towards. Most of my athletes put their names on a poster that I made, attaching themselves to actual miles of the course at Boston. I had spent four years with some of them, and this plan would form a connection between them and me as I was attempting to run the 26 miles. Heartbreak Hill was reserved for Dad. He was very instrumental in my going to college. Back when I was experiencing all those recruiting difficulties, I had become frustrated and just said I would forget the whole thing. He simply said, no, I would be going to college somewhere. I wanted to use his courage, his attitude, to conquer the most difficult portion of the race. The finish line was reserved for my mother, who had endured for fifty years the hardships and challenges of being a dairy farmer's wife. Now she was seeing her husband through the most difficult time they would ever need to deal with. I needed her with me on the way to the finish line.

Back to my training schedule, I logged fifty miles the last week in February. I followed that with three more 50+ mile weeks during the first weeks in March. I ran most every day, lots of days doing doubles with three or four miles in the morning and five miles or so at night. I did my first twenty-one miler on March 17th,, which was a unique way to spend St. Patrick's day, and jump started me to two weeks of 80 miles each. My March mileage totaled out at 267 miles. That set me up well for the taper, and I felt I was ready to take on the 100th annual Boston Athletic Association Marathon. I had chosen to race competitively very little, but along with mileage, I had done quite a few repeat 800's and several good hill workouts. All totaled I had logged 439 miles so far in 1996, and now it was time for the biggest 26 mile starting line of my life.

With all of the hype and the articles surrounding the fact that this historic race was 100 years old, the entire running world and the country were aware and excited about such a famous race. The race committee changed some things from the usual format, and allowed many more runners than ever before to take the Patriot's Day trek from Hopkinton to Boston. I had done the training, I was very healthy, and I had a huge desire to go east and do well. I felt I was ready to join the 35,000 people in a positive way and hoped I had the courage to meet this new challenge. Thinking of the challenge my father was facing, I remembered an August day when we had shared a powerful experience together.

I was probably about fourteen years old and we had been working outside. The day had been a hot, sticky, sultry one where you could work up a sweat by just walking across the yard. Things got really strange that late afternoon day. The mild breeze disappeared, the sky became a strange color of yellowish gray, and we knew things did not look good. Weather on a farm can always be a threat, and our early August crops were looking great. A strong storm could certainly ruin the possibility for an upcoming rewarding financial return for all of our hard work.

The radio told us to seek shelter and Mom and the family were in the basement. Dad and I stood out by the steps that faced the west and watched the menacing storm develop, having no business in the world being there. The clouds became even stranger and were literally rolling over and around each other, we knew it was a mixture that could cause some serious problems. The wind came first, followed by a warm sprinkle, and then things started to bust loose. The threatening lightning and thunder were awesome, almost continuous, and it was raining hard. Then we saw the tornado! It was coming right at us from the southwest, but still we stood there and watched, we watched it approaching, we moved closer to the door of the house. When it was about three-fourths of a mile away, my Dad and I saw a miraculous sight: As it reached a gravel intersection of roads, it suddenly changed its course! It turned and followed the road directly to the east, just lifting itself up and returning to the skies. Wow, our land, our crops, and our buildings had been spared. Dad and I both knew how fortunate we were, and we just stood there in awe. We both knew we had witnessed something amazing and we didn't say a word. We realized the tremendous power that we had just experienced, and we knew it was a good day to be safe. Later the family would talk about how blessed we were that the tornado had taken a different route.

My hope for the 100th annual Boston was to have some of that same courage and positive wonder as I put my body on that starting line.

Lesson learned: We never know what direction our lives will go. You can do all the planning in the world, but sometimes we are not in control. Whatever comes our way, we need to believe we can handle things and we need to have the courage to continue.

18

BOSTON #2, WITH COURAGE- COURAGE TO LIVE LIFE, CONQUER HEARTBREAK HILL, AND EVERYTHING IN BETWEEN!

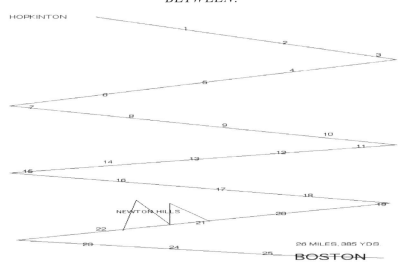

I had made my decision and stayed committed to running 26 miles from Hopkinton to Boston for the second time in my life. Having discussed this with my track team, I made the above chart as one thing to share with them. They attached their names to various miles on the above map and I carried this in my briefcase as my wife and I left home for the Minneapolis airport. We stopped in to see Mom and Dad, had lunch with some of the family, and exchanged hugs which had taken on new meaning in our lives. My parents were excited for me and wished me well. I think my trip to Boston was a welcome diversion to the uncertain, stressful times they were going through. Securing lodging in a distant, big city is always interesting. Our motel seemed fine, but it was a bit farther from downtown that we thought, therefore causing some extra planning. The day before the race, we drove the course, considering it had been seventeen years since I first had the pleasure of running those same 26 miles. Along the way we found a quaint, out of the way, restaurant that looked to be perfect for my pre-race dinner. It was relaxing, located in a semi-rural area, had a very adequate pasta menu, and was a perfect way to spend the evening. Things were calm, peaceful, and even though we were parked along the marathon course, I was very content. We finished driving most of the course leading up to the downtown area, then headed back to the motel.

The motel was catering to the marathon crowd, and the next morning it had a carbohydrate breakfast all prepared for us. The only problem was every single table in the restaurant was occupied. A young man and a lady nicely invited us to join them. During the course of conversation we learned they were both singles who just happened to be eating together. The conversation came around to qualifying times, and we learned something new about Boston. The guy shared with us the fact that he was employed by a corporation in Texas which had "purchased" his entry form. This was a bit of a surprise, having often been a part of the qualifying time dilemma. Evidently, everyone running the race did not have a qualifying time. I supposed it was just one more thing to learn about the real world, but we found that to be quite interesting.

After a couple of hours of quiet time I did more hydrating and began to dress for the race. We drove a couple of miles over to the subway parking area and took the next car to downtown Boston. Once again, I found myself on a bus full of runners, riding out to Hopkinton for the noon race start. It was a nice cool day, the sun was out, and there was a lot of excitement in the air. The ride out to the start seemed very long. It felt as though we were driving an awfully long way, and my brain started to rationalize that it was too far to run. I realized that we were taking the freeway, and it was farther around. Hey, they know how to measure and the distance will be 26 miles. I reassured myself that I was ready to run and to do it well.

The starting area had changed a lot since 1979. A big part of it was they had accepted many more entries because it was the 100th annual race, allowing more people to be a part of it. There were huge covered areas made up of various colored tents and the longest lines of port-a-pots I had ever seen. There were plenty of open spaces to stretch and relax, and they were ready for the huge crowd. I headed to the "starting area" which was different than any I had ever experienced because it went on for many blocks. There were corrals set up for all the different predicted final times. I went to the three-hour area figuring it was a fair and appropriate place to start the race. There were already several discarded pieces of clothing hanging from the fences and trees, but I held on to my extra shirt until the race actually started. It was a great place to be, sharing the starting line with 35,000 people for the 100th historic Boston Athletic Association Marathon.

The gun finally fired and I started to walk. Oops, maybe too far back. It took way too long to get to the actual starting line, and even though that first mile is almost all downhill, it also took too long before I could actually run at full stride. Then it all hit me: my sick father, almost six months of training, another flight to Boston, and I was now part of probably the most historic race ever in America. I was psyched. I was not happy to see my first mile split being slower than eight minutes, but I needed to process that and understand it was inevitable because of how the race had started. By mile two I was back in the range where I wanted to be and had twenty-four miles to go. I had thrown my extra shirt off when I had switched from walking to a slow jog. The weather was very comfortable and the mass of humanity was moving towards downtown Boston. We were getting close to mile three, and the road was still very congested. Usually by now, a person has free choice of where to run and you don't feel crowded. The farther I ran, the more this crowded feeling seemed to surround me. Somewhere around mile five I was jostled and bumped to the point I almost fell. I responded by telling myself I needed to stay focused, pay attention, and not allow myself to be so distracted. It wasn't even a mile later when my elbow was hit by someone's hand and I actually became angry. My splits were not dropping to the level I was hoping for and the constant maneuvering was getting old.

When I reached the next aid station I actually stepped between the tables and took two full cups of water. I drained them both and carefully stepped out from between the tables and continued down the road. It was time for an attitude adjustment. I needed to examine the situation. Where was the courage I was supposed to be having for this day? Which team member was I thinking about to get me through the next mile? I was still nine miles from Heartbreak Hill and I was having doubts. I reluctantly gave up on some of the time goals I had set. I was forty-three years old and no matter how well my training had gone, and no matter how much I desired to break three hours, it wasn't going to happen on April 16th of 1996. However, that didn't mean I couldn't run well and couldn't have a good run.

The new focus seemed to help. Perhaps the fact that the running field was partially thinning out was also helping. I felt like my training was beginning to make the miles go by easier, and I discovered my strength and courage as I passed people along the way. My splits were not that much over seven minutes a mile, and significant progress was coming my way.

Being a student of the game is just as an important part of running as it is for any other sport. I knew the significance of Heartbreak Hill. I found myself at the bottom of the first hill, and I was feeling strong. The temperature continued to rise, and the day began to take its toll on a few people. But I continued to pass. My dedication and commitment to keeping my father's life in my mind for the series of three hills was working well. As many people struggled and some even walked the hills, I felt strong. I found other aggressive people to pace with, and I continued to pass quite a few runners. The hills were big, but not huge. I knew they were not something to be taken lightly, however. They come at perhaps the worst point in the marathon if you are not prepared for them. I concentrated on Dad and the many hill repeats I had run all spring on a series of four hills. When I finally reached the top of Heartbreak Hill, I was still feeling strong. I remember rising over the crest, knowing that seven good miles were left in my body. I kept my conservative control for the next mile, and then I decided it was time to race the last six miles.

There is a cobblestone street section of the race that really made me wonder both in 1979 and then in 1996. I have never been a smooth stepper in terms of dealing with uneven terrain. Stairs, rail road tracks, snow covered roads, and anything that makes me pick my steps carefully seemed to be extra hard for me. I once again found myself demanding that I focus on the moment, as I gingerly picked my way over the bricks. These bricks were not going to cause me not to finish the race. And they didn't. Completing that portion, I began my personal attack on the finish line of the 100th annual Boston Marathon. My joy and my focus revolved around my mom and the support we had always given each other. With each turn, I was hoping to see the finish area, and when I finally did make the final turn, reality hit my brain. It was, indeed, a great feeling. The last few miles had gone very well, the light blue and gold banners of the BAA were very apparent, and I was very pleased to once again experience success in Boston, Massachusetts.

100TH ANNUAL
BOSTON MARATHON MEDAL

Lesson learned: When things don't appear to be going as planned, we need to figure out how to make the best of the situation!

19

"AFTER PARTY"

FINISHER

BOSTON MARATHON
April 15, 1996
Marathon Foto

(Photo provided by and used with permission of Marathon Foto.)

I had just crossed the finish line in the biggest race of my life and it felt fantastic. Now for reality: how to regroup and figure things out? I was meandering, feeling fine but pleasantly exhausted, and my dear wife found me almost immediately. I sometimes don't know how she does it. She pointed out to me where they were taking photos at a special location, so we waited in line to do that and then made our way over to the bag area. She had brought me something to put on, but the bag system was quite efficient with many volunteers helping out, and I also found my other clothes quite quickly. It was rather amazing considering the thousands of people who needed their bags.

I really felt like sitting down, so we sat and took in a few of the sights. Deb mentioned she had walked by the "Cheers" bar during her wait, and after a brief discussion, we decided to walk over there for a celebratory beer! We were actually able to get in the crowded establishment, and I drank a beer and we shared an order of onion rings. My food choices were not very healthy, but I was feeling awesome both mentally and physically and they both tasted great at the time. We relaxed and discussed the happenings of the day. We probably sat there for 45 minutes and then slowly walked out and back up the stairs to the streets of Boston. We walked the couple of blocks back to the finish line and watched some more people finish the marathon. Finish lines of 26 mile races are always interesting. After learning what I had at breakfast that morning, it makes sense that some runners there are not actual qualifiers. That is maybe part of why there were still plenty of people finishing way beyond the qualifying times. Some people probably chose to just cover the course for the experience, but whatever the reason, there were still lots of runners coming in around the 4:30 time.

When I realized it was getting close to the time the awards ceremony would be starting at a nearby motel, my wife and I walked over to check it out. We found the ballroom where it was being held and settled into chairs somewhere in the middle of the room. Like everything else about the Boston Marathon, this, too, was done very well. It was one of the many years where the Kenyan men had performed very well, and the whole ceremony was very interesting. My most curious observation was seeing the circle of winners gathered in the motel lobby as we were leaving. The Kenyan contingent was standing in a circle visiting. Several of them had the cut glass award sitting on the floor in front of them, and even though they were speaking their native language, it was easy to detect that they were very happy with the finish award checks they had in their pockets. They had once again dominated the top places and no doubt were pleased with the recent addition of prize money at the Boston Marathon.

Following the awards ceremony, we found the subway station, went down the stairs on my sensitive legs, stepped through the open, sliding door, and found a seat. There weren't any nauseous feelings like post-race in 1979, therefore, we were having a pleasant ride. My mind left the non-caring euphoria of a marathon finish, and I realized we had made a mistake. We were on the wrong subway line! We checked out some more information, and realized that our mistake was not too serious. According to the map we could ride this line to the end of it, walk two blocks over, and catch the other subway line we needed to get to our rental car. We were not in a hurry, we weren't flying out until the next day, so we just dealt with the situation. However, once we got off and started walking, we didn't see the other subway station. It was dusk in a big city with the air was starting to chill, and I was wondering where we were exactly. I went up to a lady in a sweat suit and asked if she knew where the subway station was. Her response was a question for me: "I am not sure, but do you know if I am still on the Boston Marathon course?" Wow, did I feel terrible. I had finished about four hours ago, all marathon personnel were long gone, and she was still trying to finish the 26 miles! I did look to my left and realized the road was the one leading to downtown and I assured her that yes, I thought she was on the right road. That certainly put the day in perspective. I decided my 3 hour and 12 minute time was just fine and I hoped she would find her way. We finally discovered the subway station about half a block away and made it back to our car and our motel.

The next day we went to the airport, turned our car back to the rental company, and headed into the terminal. I bought a paper to read on the flight and we began our airport wait for our plane to begin loading. Getting off the ground to head back home is always a little nerve racking, especially for my wife, but we had a smooth take off. After leveling off and getting relaxed, I began to read about the great Monday event, the Boston Marathon on Patriots' Day in Boston. I read the articles and started to examine the results pages. Sure enough, there I was finishing 5,024th out of 35,000 runners. Somehow I again felt very proud of what I was able to accomplish. To be a small part of so much running history at Boston was special. The next item the paper explained was how crowded the race had been. I realized my good buddy from back home had finished four seconds ahead of me, eleven places ahead of me, and I never saw him! Wow, that seemed just about unbelievable. He claims I beat him because he had started way up from where I was, actually several blocks, and my actual running time was faster. We were both extremely pleased we were able to have the experience of successfully running in the 100th Boston Marathon.

Lesson learned: Big, famous marathons can be amazing to experience. If you ever get the chance, go, experience what running world has to offer. We work hard, we deserve it.

O

O

20

O

O

MARATHON MATH: 20 + 6 = 26
(WHO REALLY CARES ABOUT 385 YARDS?)

I am married to a math expert. She has been a teacher for over thirty years and has taken every math class our local college has to offer. She probably wouldn't agree with my calculations, but I have come to believe that **20 is half of 26**. Of course I am referring to miles and personally how I like to approach the marathon distance.

Two factors important to race strategy are training and health. If both of these factors are more or less in perspective, the idea that half way is twenty miles has been a good approach for me. One thing it does is keep me conservative. You train for months for some of these things and it can be difficult to emotionally and mentally have things "right" at the beginning of the race. At my age the hype of traveling and the gun going off should not over excite me, but it still does. Downhill starts, beautiful mornings, and excitable racing crowds can throw things off. Sometimes you can correct mistakes after hearing a few of the mile splits, but if you don't keep it controlled, you might find yourself soaking in a lake at seventeen miles instead of at the finish line.

The racing strategy that works the best for me and was used effectively in the 1996 Boston race, is to run conservatively until the twenty mile mark, then let it go. Sometimes it really feels like I am holding back, but maybe that is a good thing. I suppose if I were a more talented runner and a real speedster, I might race it differently. On the other hand, I have approached many races in this controlled way and have still kept my splits quite even throughout the entire race. It also sets up well for negative splitting, running the second half of the race faster than the first, if things go well. Many quality and very successful races are run using the negative split concept.

Pacing myself on a realistic level for twenty-six miles is always interesting.

Experienced runners certainly have an idea how fast they think they will be able to run at any given time, just from their training. An effective strategy is not to have one specific goal, but rather a set of goals in your mind before getting ready to race. The first goal is, of course, to make it to the finish line, the second one is to finish and feel strong at the end. The third goal might be finish in a realistic time, and the fourth is to have a very quality time. Making any mistakes or miscalculations early may decide which goal is most appropriate for that day. By holding back and not letting go and running freely and aggressively until the 20 mile mark, the over all chances of success for the day are quite a bit higher. This has worked well for me in most of the marathon stories I have been telling you about. One prevailing thought that encourages that approach is "there is no wall". Much has been written about hitting the wall in the marathon. Any time you attempt to run that far, there is the possibility that you might not make it to the end. One phenomenal runner friend of mine, Karen, has only once failed to finish a single marathon in more than 20 attempts. Personally, it has not gone consistently that well for me. Sometimes I have finished and I have not been able to do much more than lay down, sometimes I have been able to dance the night away. I really think it has the most to do with how the body is responding on that given day and how well prepared the runner happens to be.

A big part of what determines how well the finish works, reflects on how well you know yourself in the last few miles of a marathon. I do believe that with proper training most runners can always run ten kilometers. Therefore if you look at the twenty mile mark as being half way, and you stay conservative, you only will have a 10k remaining to finish the day's work. Usually, if you reach that point and are doing fine, the rest of the race can really be a positive experience. This is especially true if you are feeling well enough to be a little aggressive. It also helps if the event is large enough so you can find several people to race and hopefully pass. As sick as it sounds, it is one way to stay motivated. I have sometimes been able to keep the pace solid and even drop my mile times; at that point in the race, it feels good to go past people. Granted, some are in extreme distress and maybe even have stopped to stretch or are walking, but being able to pass them does help me to get to the finish line. When this strategy works out because you made a good plan, you are able to follow it successfully to the finish.

There is a lure, an unknown reward, or perhaps a stigma to being a marathon finisher. It is not something to be taken lightly. When running becomes something to crave, it logically follows for some people to extend that into running 26 miles. Sometimes I have wondered about those that take a really long time to finish the run, but as long as it is right for them, that is all that really matters. I have admired some very great racers and have a lot of respect for anyone who can maintain a fast pace for twenty-six miles in a row. If running a marathon is something you have not yet experienced, and you think it is a possibility, I would encourage you to go for it. You need to work towards it gradually, slowly working your way up to it, and it really helps to have some training partners. It is a unique feeling to complete a twenty-six mile race with much satisfaction and personal reward. Deciding, planning, training, resting and then executing the plan can be very beneficial physically and mentally. A runner can't help but have a sense of pride and accomplishment when crossing that finish line.

One of the biggest deterrents I have discovered to executing the race plan is the presence of other people that I know. That year at Grandma's Marathon that I talked about in "Mile 12", I had too many of my close friends there with me, and it was one of my worst running experiences ever. Perhaps it is more efficient to approach the activity in a more selfish manner. Getting personal feedback and understanding what our own bodies are doing is essential. If we spend too much energy worrying about others, that becomes difficult. At least it does for me. My best racing successes have occurred farthest from home, and I'm not sure why. Perhaps it is because I have been more excited about them, or I feel I have to do well because I have spent so much money to travel there, or because I know so few people. Maybe all three are factors, but those far away trips have seemed to bring about the fastest runs.

I am encouraged by the number of marathons in our nation and the number of people that are running them. It seems very healthy that women are starting to pass the men in terms of how many enter road races. That points toward a healthy equality and a positive possibility for all. Personally, with physical pains that seem to be coming up more often, I am not sure what my future marathon schedule will be. I guess future developments will determine that. I know Chicago, Drake Relays, Arizona, Washington and New York Marathons are some that I have considered. Who knows if any will happen, but it would be interesting to see some of them as either a spectator or a participant. I am sure that some year the familiar urge to take part in either the Twin Cities Marathon or Grandma's in Duluth will also jump back in my brain.

One recent experience of applying my marathon math was the Fargo Marathon, held in May of 2006 in Fargo, North Dakota. The race has been held for only a few years, and has become established as a quality, well-attended event. Fargo is a bit of a smaller city, but they do a nice job of conducting a very user-friendly race. The two sides of the cool medal are pictured above, the center rectangle actually spins and says "Far go" or "Go far" The course is also extremely flat, the only elevation changes being when you pass over or under a different roadway. My conservative approach centered around eight-minute miles. I was running this one at fifty-three years of age, and I really entered more for the experience and finding the finish line rather than to be "racing."

The race began at their convention center with the early miles winding around downtown. From there we headed south through a beautiful corridor of huge, old trees. The miles were clicking along nicely with most splits being slightly below my goal pace. As we made our way to the newer part of town on the southern end, the course followed a long cement path through a huge, modern park. When we turned and headed back to the north the wind became much stronger than I had anticipated. This part of the United States is well known for its wind, but the abrupt change surprised me. From mile eleven to mile fifteen I was fighting it and there was not a lot of company around to use for sharing the work. I proceeded along the course and still thought the day was going fine, but at about eighteen miles something really changed. We had crossed over into the sister city of Moorhead, Minnesota, and I turned right heading down a new street. At that point I SWALLOWED A BUG! It just shocked me, reflexes caused me to cough it up, and I spent a few seconds with not very much air. That seemed to be the start of a downward spiral for the day. Everything became a struggle. I was psyching for that twenty mile mark, and now it seemed to become questionable if I would even make it that far. I did get there, but my splits were slowing down. My mile times had crept up quite a bit higher than my desired eight minutes per mile.

Maybe it was one of those days where things were just not meant to be. It was also very likely the wind had taken a bit more out of me than I wanted to admit. At a little over twenty-one miles we crossed the bridge to get back to North Dakota, and I met my family. They were there with cameras in hand, and of course it wasn't the first time I had been greeted by them that day, but they knew I reached this point slower than expected. I must have not looked too strong, because my daughter asked if I needed help, and she jumped on the course to join me. It was probably not the fairest thing to do, or the proudest moment of my life, but by now I had spent several minutes walking and to make it almost five more miles to the finish was not looking good. There wasn't really anything specific bothering me, which was really a different and unique experience for me. I was just overall, genuinely sore, and I had lost most of my motivation for even caring about the finish line. She inspired me, distracted me, motivated me, and began to save the day for me. I needed to throttle her enthusiasm and keep things in control, but we kept moving through the last part of the course. We were mostly at a slow jog and we even walked a block or two. At about mile twenty-three my son decided to join the family affair, the wind was no longer a factor, and they convinced me to keep my feet moving and they really wanted their dad to finish the race. I was feeling very humble at the time and also very grateful they understood how important this was to me.

We finally took a left turn and headed back to that same convention center parking lot that I had left almost four hours earlier. The kids dropped off as I entered the parking lot, and I found my way through the lot, followed the cement barriers around the building, and finally entered the convention center. The marathon planners do an awesome job of letting the runners finish inside the Fargodome Convention Center and you get to see yourself on the jumbotron television screen as you finish the race. This was a very cool method of finishing the race, but I was more concerned about sitting down. I had once again found a marathon finish line, even though my marathon math equation had not a real positive factor for the day, but I was certainly happy I had started the race in a controlled manner. Maybe it wasn't my day, perhaps I had over trained, but it was still a very positive overall experience. I was happy I had given it my best and that I had completed the 26 miles. I really felt good about Traci and Jake helping me through the ordeal. The post race brew seemed like something I had earned, it tasted great, and I had still accomplished the 26 miles, 385 yards in 3 hours and 51 minutes.

My next door neighbor, Stephen, was the first person to read the beginning of this chapter. I was in the process of helping him prepare for the first marathon of his life. He was heading to Orlando, Florida for the Disney Marathon. We had been doing some training together and we were doing lots of visiting about what he wanted to accomplish. I will never forget the first time we ran eleven miles together. It was his longest run so far and he was extremely pleased with the effort. I also used the technique with Steve of visualizing himself at that finish line. That's another thing to use to bring about success. Steve used the techniques mentioned here, and he did get to the finish line at Epcot Center. He was smiling big and feeling that great sense of marathon accomplishment as he completed his first twenty-six miler. I hope many of you can use "marathon math" to do the same at your next marathon.

****

"THERE IS NO WALL!"

****

This is probably the best place to share my personal insight on how I prepare for a big race in terms of diet. My favorite dietary scheme does involve carbohydrate starving and carbohydrate loading. It fits in with marathon math because I use a six-day approach prior to the race.

3 Days of Protein + 3 Days of Carbohydrates = 6 Days of Preparation

Six days out I move from my general pattern of healthy eating to concentrating on eating virtually a complete protein diet. This is the most difficult and unpleasant part because the choices are limited and the three days does get a little long. Meat, milk, and eggs are the main sources to draw from, with a little nuts thrown in here and there. Snacks are the tough part, but jerky, sardines, herring, and peanuts help me get through it. I don't do 100% protein, but I am sure the rate is up there somewhere about 90%. Some of the protein drinks help, but it is still a tough three days. I will usually throw in a five or six mile higher quality run as I start this phase. All of this helps me focus on exactly what I am attempting to accomplish. It also depletes my body of those high energy carbs that it craves and I think it really sets me up to absorb those when the time comes.

The next and final three days before the race is carbohydrate time. The closer I get to race time I eat a higher concentration of carbs. My wife is a great supporter of what I do, and she will even ask which particular meals I would like on which days. Pastas, pizzas, breads, deserts, pastries, cereals, pancakes, French toast, waffles and all the rest of those great dishes are easy to come up with, the sum total of which gets me to the starting line with a full tank. I always seem to do fine eating a large meal of carbs the night before a race. It works well for me depending upon the race time the next day. I may have a Clif Bar or some kind of other energy bar, possibly a banana, and any juice that is high in carbohydrate content on the morning of the race. I try to take in those foods about three hours before the starting time for the race. I avoid orange juice the morning of a race, but do take in water along with the Mountain Dew energy product called "Amp". It seems to be my new favorite booster prior to going to the starting line.

In addition, I almost always use the restroom at least three times before the gun goes off. My body seems to know how to prepare for what I am about to put it through, and it does a good job of emptying out the excess contents. While bowel movements seem to follow an exact schedule, urination is never as clear cut. Hopefully I have consumed enough so the urine is clear in color, but how often and when I pee is always a gamble. One time I ran a very good marathon while I actually felt like I needed to empty my bladder most of the way. I will stop if it seems like it would be more comfortable, but it is just obviously part of the whole package and something you always hope works out well. The frequency of out-houses on most courses seems very adequate, but a good piece of advice would be to practice these things ahead of time to have a good idea how bathroom necessities will work out for you on race day. Personally, I very rarely carry any water or food with me. I do not recommend it, but in some of my early marathons, I drank or ate very little during the actual run. Recently I use the water and energy drink stops most of the time, at least every three miles if that works out in the later stages of the race. Sometimes I will take two glasses on the jog through a water stop, crease the cup, and drink both of them as I continue along the course. If the race has aid stations every two miles, I will alternate, doing water at one station and energy drink at the other. These methods and strategies have worked out in positive ways for me. Feel free to try them, and if they are different from what you are used to doing, try them for a training run or a specific workout before you use them in a race. There probably are no perfect ways of taking in liquids and solids prior to and during a race, but these are trial and error solutions that have helped me run successful marathons.

Lesson learned: "There is no wall" can be a good mantra or repetitive thing to think and say to help get you to the finish line. Find a mantra that works for you, is personal, and helps you to remain strong and keep you on pace. Things like, "I am having a good day", "I am strong", and "There is no wall that can stop me" might help improve your race.

CELEBRITIES AND RUNNING WITH DICK BEARDSLEY

Along with many of the personal, mental, and physical running challenges I have faced over the years, I have also had the privilege of meeting some of the top running personalities in our nation. The biggest opportunity for doing this has been by attending the United States Olympic Track and Field Trials. The first time we started doing this was in 1984 at the Coliseum in Los Angeles, California. My wife and I have gone to all the Trials ever since. The Track Trials are an eight-day track meet that features the best men and women runners and track athletes in America. The span of time is usually ten or eleven days and the recent meets have been in Los Angeles, New Orleans, Indianapolis, Atlanta and twice in Sacramento. For a runner or a spectator, I would highly recommend attending it. Spending eight days watching all of the events and the competition is nothing short of amazing. Compared to many sporting events, the tickets are reasonably priced. Probably the most dramatic thing is that third place becomes the important finishing spot. Sure, winning the event is still #1. Many times the winner will set a standard of one of the top performances for the year in that event, and often times they may even perform at a national or world record level. But the drama of the top three individuals qualifying for our Olympic team, and the fourth person going home, is really huge. I would like to share some highlights of those experiences over the years.

Back in 1984, the Los Angeles Coliseum was a huge place for the event, and there were plenty of spaces to spread out and move around. There was also time in the schedule to take breaks and enjoy the city. My wife really enjoys that aspect of the trips, as it keeps her hyper, overactive husband in one place for a long period of time and we get to discover lots of things about the host city. One day in LA I decided I had been sitting around too much and needed to go for a run. Running through any vacation spot is always interesting, and I see it as a great way to research the area and just another way to experience the place you are visiting. I was running alone towards downtown from the track on a medium-sized city street, just out for a run, and I meet Mary Decker-Slaney coming down the street the other way. She, of course, has held multiple American records and

dominated the women's scene for many years. Here I was running down the same street with her. It really felt weird to be out on a casual run on the same street as one of our nation's best. We did the silent wave to each other and I had a story to tell. My wife and I have always enjoyed Mary's intensity and gritty approach to competition, and she was honestly one of the best female spitters I have ever seen in my life. (Yes I know, spell check doesn't like that word, "spitters", but Mary was very good at it.)

One big part of the experience for me has been to observe how grateful and genuine many of the athletes have been. I will never forget walking behind the stadium at dusk with my two boys and noticing Steve Scott just kind of hanging out. He was standing under one of the stadium lights, and as we walked up to him, I initiated a conversation. It was amazing to walk up to the man that has broken the four-minute mile more times than any other American, and have him take the time to visit with us. He had a couple of days before the next round of competition and he was very content to thank us for coming and to visit about the trials. What an opportunity for the three of us to spend some time with such a quality individual! Steve literally wanted to spend some time just absorbing the entire trials atmosphere for himself, and he wasn't afraid to be available to the fans. He was also one of the most level-headed, humble celebrities I have ever met.

Another highlight was shaking the hand of Regina Jacobs after she had won the women's 1500 in Sacramento. She was running the victory lap around the track and came around to the backstretch. I usually like to sit on the backstretch, directly across from the finish line. There was a platform area at the bottom of the bleacher aisle and she climbed up on that to thank the fans. I had come down to get a good picture and there she was right in front of me and thirty other friends of track and field. She was wearing a huge smile and sincerely thanked the fans who had been cheering wildly as we watched her great performance. I could only think that she had the strongest, most developed arm strength I had ever seen in a woman as she shook my hand. (Unfortunately, she would later be accused of performance enhancement which I believe ended her career.)

There was also the time I met Carl Lewis walking through the crowd in Indianapolis. We both approached from different directions a walkway halfway up the seating area. He didn't give us an actual autograph, but he did hand us a signed picture of himself. Conversations with people like Bob Kennedy, Steve Holman, and Shot Putter Ron Backes, have been other memorable highlights I have experienced at the Trials.

The race director for a former duathalon (a bike/run combination) held in Bemidji, brought in celebrity runners as part of the festivities. Boston Billy, Bill Rodgers himself, was here one year for our local race. I was able to get him to autograph my 1996 Boston Marathon T-Shirt and it was amazing to stand on a quiet street corner in our home town and visit with him. I have several minutes of great video tape with Bill and several of our local runners. Once again, he was an extremely pleasant person and it was an honor to have him visit our community.

Just a mere ninety miles from Bemidji is the community of Detroit Lakes, Minnesota. One famous runner who used to reside there is Dick Beardsley. When Dick first left distance running, he used the money he had won to start a dairy farm in Minnesota. I was born and raised on a dairy farm and when you see so many famous athletes doing some showy, crazy things, I just thought it was cool that Mr. Beardsley took a more natural, environmental approach. Unfortunately, things would not work out so well for Dick. He had a serious farming accident that caused quite a major crisis in his life. As an indirect result of that accident, he became a personal acquaintance of mine. He helps promote the annual half-marathon in Detroit Lakes, and has made it possible for me and others to meet such great individuals as Joan Benoit and the great Frank Shorter. Each September he brings in a celebrity guest as part of the weekend race festivities in Detroit Lakes, Minnesota.

DICK BEARDSLEY-

It was a Thursday in January, in Bemidji, Minnesota, a rather grand day of thirty degrees when winter is not that hard to enjoy. Today though, a legend was coming to town, someone I had heard of, read about, admired, and worried about for some time. Dick Beardsley was due in town at four o'clock, and I was scheduled to meet him and to run with him. Wow, there honestly isn't too much I'd rather do on a January afternoon. The gentleman that was with me on the very first run of this book, our local health teacher, had arranged for Dick to come and talk to his classes. He had also arranged our time to run with Dick on the local indoor track.

Dick was just a few minutes late, but when my friend, Gary Mullranin, introduced us, Dick smiled instantly. Whenever you are about to run with someone, especially if that someone used to be a world class runner, you automatically start to size him up. He was trim, lean, and still looked good to go. I thought, oh boy, what have I gotten myself into now. We entered the local college indoor track area and walked over toward the end where a few college runners were stretching. Still doubting how the ensuing run would go, I lagged behind, not really sure of the day's plan. My friend introduced Dick to a few of the kids, and within minutes, twenty to twenty-five college youth sat down in front of him, and he proceeded to tell his story.

The students were in awe, totally listening, and Dick Beardsley just simply spilled his guts. Due to several misfortunes of life, a farm accident and a couple of running/automobile accidents, he had moved from world class athlete to a drug addict. Pain killers were all prescription and all "needed" for a while, but things had gotten out of hand. Through manipulation and illegal forgery, Dick started writing his own prescriptions and proceeded to reach an incredible level of drug consumption that could easily have killed him. The fake prescriptions resulted in arrest, conviction, and a huge concern over whether or not he would end up in jail. Once the fact that he was not selling the large amounts of pills to others was established, a lighter sentence was granted, and his life became his to put back together.

As with many people who have found their way out of an addictive lifestyle, Dick was overly zealous in his new excitement for life. He was glad to be alive, thrilled to be clean, and was on the track to a meaningful and positive existence. The "one day at a time" idea came through loudly and clearly. He shared two especially significant things that day. The first one was that chemical dependency can happen to anyone. Mr. Beardsley had acquired an incredible amount of insight through his struggles with addiction. He had many friends and a lot of support, but chemical dependency still took its hold. He also shared that if there are things in life you are all about and want to get to, you need to find the time and do that. He was very humble, motivational, and encouraging to the young athletes in the midst of their college running careers.

I have been instrumental in helping two people begin the treatment process for chemical dependency. It is a complicated endeavor, and I am pleased to say both of those situations resulted in eventual successes and both people are once again leading active, productive, drug free lives. Good health is as special and positive as addictive health is devastating. Whenever a person can find the way to turn things around, life teaches them a valuable lesson.

It was obvious that Dick Beardsley realized he was very fortunate, and he could talk a mile a minute, but the run was still before us. When he mentioned back surgery and how messed up the farm accident had been for his leg, he also pointed out the scar tissue and explained some of the long, slow tedious rehabilitation he had experienced. My curiosity was growing, as I still knew he had been second at Boston and had actually been one of the former winners of Grandma's Marathon.

And soon it was clear I had nothing to dread. First of all, he ran with a limp. Not a terrible one, but just sort of a hitch to his gait. But he talked, and he talked, and he talked, and we just jogged along. Along the way Dick has made a number of choices. One decision has become to run always, every day a little, and not to worry about things like races, and how fast he could still be, or any of the other unrealistic traps some of us fall into. His awesome prevailing attitude was non-stop. He was very interested in me, in others, and a he had genuine acceptance of the abundant blessings that life does eventually bring. The lap splits, the distance, the quality, were not all that important. The doing, the being able to do, and the enjoyment have become the bigger goals- not so much for each day, but for life.

Through it all, he was, and in his own way, still has remained, a winner. He was the winner against a drug addiction, the winner for life, and the winner as a story teller. We spent the rest of the evening at my friend's house for dinner and visiting. My friend Gary was also the dad of one of my most talented runners I have ever had the honor of coaching. Luke and some of my other high school runners joined us for dinner. A few college runners also were there, and several of us older community runners all spent some quality time in my friend's home with Dick Beardsley. And what an evening we had. We were actually rolling off of our chairs and holding our stomachs with the great anecdotes and descriptions that Dick was throwing our way. When asked what his favorite race of all time had been, he went into a fifteen-minute description of his Grandma's victory. His watch had failed to keep running, so he didn't know how fast he was going. He hit downtown Duluth with bicyclists flanking him and he ran smack, dab into a small child that had wandered out onto the road. How did he put it, "The child froze like a deer stuck in your headlights." That is one of those expressions that northern Minnesotans can really relate to. He thought the finish clock wasn't working because he saw 2 hours and zero some minutes as he approached it. Running a 2:08 was an awesome performance, and winning Grandma's Marathon in Duluth, Minnesota over local favorite Gary Bjorklund was indeed a great day. That afternoon and evening at my friend's home was one of the biggest highlights of all of my running experiences

I am extremely happy that Dick was able to get the help he needed and to find the strength and the wisdom to discover a way of life without drugs. He continues to tell his story and to run. His times are slowly dropping and he is willing to share his recovery story with anyone who will listen. Things have continued to improve, and he has recently opened a running store in nearby Fargo, North Dakota. He also had the honor of being the spokesperson for the 2008 and 2009 Grandma's Marathon.

Parts of this book have been written over several years. Spending five hours with Dick Beardsley inspired me, pushed me, and helped me to focus on something new. Our time on this earth is not limitless. Dick said that if there were things in life we were meant to do and had been putting off, it would probably make sense to get at them. That evening while driving home, I realized I was meant to complete this book on running. I feel running has shaped my life to help make me what I am today. Not that running was the only thing, or even the most important thing, but just that it meant enough to me that I wanted to take this opportunity to share it with others. One message of the book points towards enjoying life on the run. Hopefully, by sharing some of the moments I have experienced through running, you might make sense of your life and your running. Sometimes I have been dedicated, sometimes I have been fast, but for the past forty plus years I have always been a runner. I am fortunate to have had people like Dick Beardsley and others in my life who have inspired me to continue down that running road.

Lesson learned: Enjoy life on the run. If there are important things in your life you have been putting off, find the time to get after them.

STOP RUNNING TO DIRECT A RACE

Dear Race Director, (a special Christmas letter)

I was going to write to you right after this summer's race, but this actually seems to be a more appropriate time of the year to share our story with you- You and your family seem dedicated to physical fitness, so hearing about people getting healthy is not any big revelation, but my husband and I started our journey to our fitness goals 8 months and 18 months respectively prior to the Tutto Bene race last summer. No Atkins, no South Beach, no personal trainers, no health club- just eating better food, smaller portions and walking every day! A special co-worker convinced me to enter your race, and though I never expected him to agree, both hubby and I registered for the 10k. By race day, we had shed 75#s and 45#s respectively, which totaled 120#s- almost another person! We were excited and apprehensive, but we walked the 10k route, and to our surprise and delight, we were not last...

Rubbing elbows with the seasoned runners, we were surprised how friendly people seemed and how encouraging they were. Even during the awards ceremony, we appreciated you mentioning the "walkers" as well as runners- because not everyone can run, even if they would like to...

This is just to say that as first time participants in the Tutto Bene race, we were proud to be a small part of it, and found that the people involved in your event at least, are not snobs- they seem glad you are putting forth the effort. We now understand that participating in this kind of event has not so much to do with whether or not you cross the finish line first, but more about your own goals, and achieving your personal best- which we did!

So, thanks again for the hard work and hours you invest each year, and the treats served afterwards- super fruit! Hopefully, we can do it again next year-!

An extension of my personal running and my athletic coaching is being race director for the most successful road race in our area. We have had a continued increase in participation for over a fourteen year stretch. I actually directed the race prior to that time in a little different format, so really, we have now been conducting the race for over twenty years.

2007 T SHIRT ART FOR TUTTO BENE RUN

Our race is actually a double race featuring a two mile and ten kilometers. From the above letter you realize it is totally welcomed to either run or walk the races, or perhaps a combination of the two. It has been a joy and an honor to conduct this race. My wife has been involved every year and my children have helped on race day, or they have actually raced several times. It really is "our" race and it is something we enjoy conducting every 4th of July. We call it the Tutto Bene 10k and the Cabin Coffeehouse 2 mile. Individual plaques are handed out to the winners and we've done awards in different classes and quantities over the years. We have a nice contingent of annual workers, the local JC's let us hold the race in conjunction with their water carnival, and our local Italian Ristorante, called "Tutto Bene", and a coffee house called "The Cabin" are the prime sponsors. We actually used to be part owners of the Italian restaurant, and we still have some close connections.

Being a long time distance running coach and also one of the regular runners in our community helps make the race successful. We also try to cater to everyone, encouraging group and family entries, and making it a very user-friendly day for all involved. People get the positive experience of a well-planned race on a beautiful summer day in Bemidji, Minnesota. We are fortunate to be able to block off part of the downtown area; therefore we can have a relaxed start and finish right on the streets. This also allows us to start and finish next to the restaurant and the coffeeshop, which is slightly downhill and runs towards Paul Bunyan, Babe, and Lake Bemidji.

Our record is 374 runners! I am sure that some day we could surpass 500 registrations if all of the right people were in town at the right time. It is not all about the numbers, but it is about allowing as many people as possible to have the experience. Whether it is a one time thing for someone or a person who runs the race every year, the full acceptance of who they are is always the same. Some very non-athletic individuals, couples, and groups have been a part of the race. For this reason we present awards to everyone who covers the distance. It seems most consistent with our overall race philosophy. The runners and walkers can come out, get some exercise, and enjoy a morning of moving down the road with a huge group of people who literally fill the street one block from the famous "Paul Bunyan and Babe the Blue Ox". The book front cover photo, provided compliments of a ski fanatic at skinnyski.com, captures the atmosphere created by our race.

Both before and after the race, I attempt to be very available through telephone, mail, and computer. We try to get people relaxed and comfortable about coming out and covering the distance. Lots of them have doubts, so I make it a point to encourage them in a very positive way. We try to emphasize the act of running the race as opposed to timing or placing. After all, in any race, only one person is going to be the first across the finish line. That hardly means that the thousands of others that are out there doing it aren't just as important. This doesn't mean that the race is not competitive or that we don't have quality performances. Our records are 10:10 for men and 11:10 for the women in the two mile and 34:07 and 37:10 for the ten kilometer. Two of these are held by former athletes that I have coached. There are lots of people that just come to enjoy the day. They walk with their friends or relatives, and one special group of three girls comes every year dressed up in crazy costumes.

Life that involves an occasional walk, jog, or run is simply a better life. You breathe faster, you improve your muscle tone, you exchange a lot of new fresh air, and you very often experience people on a whole different level. Sometimes when you are in charge of athletic activities you don't get a chance to realize the meaning and importance of what you do. The letter that starts this chapter expresses it well. Many people do mention it, acknowledge it, crave it, and thank us for the opportunity to do it. Once a person makes the commitment and actually gets up and gets on the line to do it, there will always be a way to see it in a positive way. Even if things don't go perfectly for everyone, chances are life is still better because they did it.

The messages in this chapter show how one race can impact an individual, perhaps for a lifetime. The extension of that first race is when some people go out and race many additional times. The repetitive experience carries running to a higher level and brings on a whole new realm of positive rewards. Physical benefits continue to multiply as a runner gradually gets in better shape. The workload and dedication can give a person such positive feedback that the sum total of all that happens literally changes a person for life. I could admit that some people, like myself, carry this concept to the extreme and that we actually become addicted to endurance running. Our minds start to value repeating the activity, and we yearn to experience it on a regular basis. Like anything we crave or desire, we simply find ourselves making sure we continue to get out and experience it.

Besides the physical and mental benefits, another huge piece is the social activity that goes along with running. No matter where you travel, if going out for a run or entering a race, it is just about impossible not to become acquainted with another runner. We like to share. We all experience many of the same things, and we know that many of us are more alike than we are different. That is probably why we run together, plan workouts together, and encourage each other to keep enjoying the running life. Sometimes the meeting of others is very informal and strictly a one-time thing. That doesn't even seem to matter among runners. I have shared and learned things about runners that are really quite intimate and important, without even knowing the other person's name. There just seems to be a lot of honesty and trust that goes along with what we all do that makes it easy to form those special bonds.

Most important, are the running friends that become such an intricate part of what we do. Some of the people have changed throughout the years, but there seems to always be those who are ready for a Saturday morning over distance run or a nice easy Sunday jog. Currently my running partners are my former assistant coach, my business partner, and my neighbor. Throughout my lifetime there have always been running friends to share the load. They help to make sure that the next speed workout really happens or that the weekly mileage goal is accomplished. One friend used to be notorious for being at my bedroom window, knocking on it to wake me up, so we would get that run taken care of before anything else happened for the day. These friends are life-long running comrades no matter if you still actually run together or not. Once you have shared the road, done the work together, probably spilled your guts about a thing or two, and maybe even run a race together, you are connected in a unique way that is difficult to explain to someone who doesn't run. There are just times when you connect and/or re-connect because you once shared something very meaningful.

The Tutto Bene race and the many others I have attended are indeed a social gathering. Many of us arrive early and share stories of having been at the same race before or learn about race specifics if we are there for the first time. We also touch base once again with old and new training partners. Most running people are very willing to share what their feelings are before they run or their plans for the day. During the race a few folks visit along the way, and others tend to keep very quiet. Regardless of flowing conversation or quiet concentration, there is still the social gathering of experiencing the activity together. Somehow knowing we are all doing the same thing, running the same course, and working our bodies in similar ways, it gives us an undeniable connection.

Post-race sharing and visiting are probably the most meaningful times spent together. Relief, accomplishment, happiness, survival and contentment are a few of the emotions that are usually part of the after-race atmosphere. Hanging around the finish line, the food stations facility, and the awards area just about always brings about several conversations. Runners certainly visit with friends and acquaintances, and even with total strangers. After finishing a race runners tend to feel like sharing and reflecting on the experience with others. Occasionally, sharing a meal or an adult beverage continues the social gathering and the relaxed reflection time.

These are some of the reasons why I am motivated to continue hosting this race. We willingly give many hours every year to this community activity and we are privileged to provide this opportunity for others. Some days I think it is too much work and sometimes over the years there have been frustrations to be dealt with. Occasionally, a person will take one incident that happened during their day and complain about it. I try to be objective and not let those negative things bother me. But then a letter like the one starting this chapter or the following letter arrives and puts everything into true perspective. These experiences are very important for anyone who chooses to be a part of the runner's racing life. Whether you are a part of it because you are an entrant, a worker, or even an observer, I can almost guarantee you will see some positive, cool things. What could be better?

Dear Mr. Bartz,

Thank you so much for running such a wonderful run on the 4th of July. It is the second year I've run it in its current format. The Jaycee Water Carnival 10k- its predecessor I think- was the first 10k I had ever done when I was 12 (years old). The run started a love of running which continues to this day. I love the race you run! This year I talked both my cousin and my aunt into doing your 10k. It was my cousins first 10k. Hopefully she gets the running bug. Thanks again for such a great event!

Lesson learner: Giving time and energy for others can allow them to see life in a new way and perhaps improve their quality of life for years to come.

It was a Saturday in November and 12 or more Bemidji runners were racing in the cities. There was snow on the ground last week and 8 of our kids were still outside running. In September we practiced in the state park on a Saturday, we met an ex runner from the 80's out there all alone, she was still running on the trails 20 years after being on the team. On the way home I saw another runner on South Lake Irvine out doing the same thing. In October an old Lumberjack runner from St. Cloud called, his 7 year old son was quite hyper that evening so they went out and jogged 4 blocks together. This year we had 5 running parent's children on the BHS CC team. I am humbled to have shared the gift with so many people. Wins and losses are fun to look at, but adopting running as an ingredient of character for a lifetime is awesome. I wonder how many people get out on a weekend and jog, run, or even race because they have spent time with Bemidji Cross Country? I'm sure on some occasions it is in the hundreds. Thank you for accepting and sharing the gift. May it serve you well, now, and perhaps, for a lifetime.

Dennis "Barny" Bartz, Head Bemidji Cross Country Coach– 1981-2007

Well, it is official. At 54 years of age I have withdrawn from my third, and perhaps final, head coaching position. I am very proud of my career and the things I have been able to accomplish. There have been bumps in the road and a few situations where I became very nervous about how things might work out. However, the overall feeling is that coaching was great. I know I have affected many people throughout the years, and I know I have helped numerous people to become more positive, confident, and productive individuals.

This year, as in so many from the past, we began the season with a team member finishing last in an early season race. One year a girl that had just joined the team put it this way, "I was so embarrassed I wanted to have a brown paper bag over my head." This year as well as in that situation, the person came around to doing just fine. All at once they would find themselves having a half dozen or so folks finishing behind them. Their confidence starts to grow, they start to feel better about themselves as a runner, and positive feelings continue to bring about positive results. Soon they are finding themselves in the middle of the pack, and sometimes within a year of so, they even work their way into winning a ribbon or a medal. Sure, it is probably in a junior varsity race, but they have become a runner. The man I am very strongly recommending become my replacement was actually one of my former runners. He was a junior varsity runner and he couldn't make our varsity team when he was in high school, but he went on to do quite well at college and to become a successful road racer as he matured and learned how to train and compete. (He did become the head coach and I assisted him for 2 years.)

It is probably most important that we give ourselves a chance to get after things and work hard at whatever comes our way. As a country boy I occasionally made it to the favorite swimming lake and we would frequently drive a half mile at the end of the day to jump in the local river and cool off. There was no formal swimming instruction and the actual competitive swimming strokes were only something we watched on television. I had very little fear of water and I could survive in deep water and swim long distances through a variety of made up techniques. For some reason the side stroke was always my strongest weapon.

Somehow, I think begging and looking pathetic were part of it, I passed the required swimming components of a Physical Education major. So how in the world did I walk into my teaching job and become a swimming coach? Of course it was through friends, friends who believed in me, and friends who recognized I would be willing to work hard at learning what I needed to learn. After five very good years of middle school swim coaching, I applied and was named the new varsity swimming coach. I paralleled many things I had learned through track and cross country and applied all the same training techniques to swimming. Along the way there were coaches, clinicians, and practical assistants that would prove to be very helpful. The biggest discovery and strongest point that made me successful, was that I learned by training in the water there was less resistance and stress on the body and I could work my swimmers at an intense level every day. I used this knowledge to coach my team to the highest winning point difference in history at the regional tournament and then resigned from that sport. The biggest reason for stopping was that I was coaching all year round and child number three had entered our family life. It was simply time to pay more attention to my wife and children.

Perhaps my coaching career would have not lasted for 34 years if I didn't have the honor of coaching 2 of our children in my programs. By the time they went through their middle school and high school teams it didn't seem to make any sense to not keep coaching. Watching them grow and mature and come to value what they were able to accomplish was one of the most special things I have ever done. Some of their best friends were also part of the program and seeing all that help our teams to be the best they could be was truly special. The positive connections and constant improvements were always sufficient rewards to keep me motivated to do my best. As big as that if not bigger, was that I was almost always able to motivate my athletes to also do their best. I would say there were possibly 2 or 3 years in my whole career where that was not the case, and those groups of athletes were simply not all that coachable. It made for long seasons, but it also really made me appreciate the good ones. Considering the good side of the extreme, my teams performed so well during two seasons that I was awarded the highest honor a coach can receive in the state of Minnesota. They selected me as the Minnesota Boys Cross Country Coach of the Year in 1984 and the Minnesota Girls Cross Country Coach of the Year in 1996. We, as a team and a coach, make up crazy sayings, we design silly and serious t-shirts, and somehow we become a very close team.

This final season was certainly one of the best fall coaching seasons, and one of the most together teams, I have had. I have been quite active in my church over the course of a lifetime, and one special aspect of this last season of being head coach had to do with being able to coach an athlete that I watched grow up in our church. Andy was just a joy and a pleasure to work with every single day. His small, coy smile was always quick to come to his face and he gradually became a very dedicated runner. He had spent time with baseball and basketball over the years. His father, who is actually an ordained pastor and chaplain of our local hospital, had been a basketball nut for most of his life. Andy gradually discovered through Cross Country that his truest talent really was in his running, and he also joined the track team the spring of his junior year. He spent his last year and a half of high school with an educated approach to full time running and he obtained some very positive results. He also became a quiet, determined, dedicated leader and many others followed his footsteps. It was just great to see Andy qualify as our third runner for the 2007 state CC meet, but then totally awesome to see him lead our team at that state meet and finish 34th in the whole state of Minnesota

Working with a large group of young male and female runners is very rewarding. We seem successful at forming a bond that is very powerful and very supportive. Most years the new runners that join our team come as a result of hearing how great the experience has been in the past. Sure, it is not for everyone, but almost anyone who completes a season is back for every season available for them until they graduate. We require that everyone accepts all of those they run with, regardless of ability, and I think that is just a good understanding for life. We come in different shapes and sizes and different abilities, and all of that is ok.

Along with that I have coached some very successful people. Many of them were regional champions and lots of our athletes have competed very well at the Minnesota State level. When I think of them and their past and future successes I am very proud of what they have accomplished. It is also very exciting to see them continue to find success at the collegiate or citizen level of racing and competing.

Troy was a smooth, strong runner. He was very quiet, he had been one of the best football prospects in our school in the ninth grade, and then he came out for cross country. That, along with his track background, combined to make him a very successful 800 meter athlete. He ended up setting our school record of 1:55.8 and then he didn't run in college. At the time I was very disappointed. Several years later I found myself about 3 rows deep toward the start of a 10k starting line and I was getting mentally prepared to run a good race. I stretched a bit, checked my watch to make sure it was in stopwatch mode and cleared to 0:00, and we were off. I took about 20 good strides and there was Troy right along side of me. I was very surprised and genuinely happy to see him. He was home for our local race this summer and we were also both entered in the local triathlon this passed August. He is very fit, placed high in both events, and is looking great.

Out most successful collegiate athlete has got to be Luke Mullranin. Luke was also quiet, but tenaciously dedicated to be the best he could be and about as humble as any athlete I have ever coached. This is not to say he wasn't intentional and serious about running. He is one of about a dozen Bemidji High School runners that I coached to a sub 4:25 mile. He led our Cross Country Team to a 7th place and a 4th place team finish and in his senior year he was the 4th fastest runner in the state of Minnesota. Speaking of our great state, he went on to run for the Minnesota Gophers and culminated his career there by becoming the most valuable runner for the Cross Country team in his senior year. He led the team at CC nationals but found even more success on the track. During his senior year he finished second in the Big 10 Track and Field Meet in the Steeple Chase and he just missed qualifying for the Olympic Trials.

Stacey, the first girl I coached that broke our high school 800 meter record, went on to be a Collegiate Conference Champion in Cross Country for Adams State in Colorado. She was also a National Champion in Division II for the 800. A few years later I had the honor of watching Marie, another former runner who was running for the University of North Dakota, achieve the same honor in Division II Nationals in the 800.

Our next and current record holder of the Bemidji 800 meter standard, Rebekah, followed Stacey to Adams State and also had a great career competing for them. She culminated her career, becoming a steeple chaser, by missing qualifying for the Olympic Trials in Sacramento, California by one person.

There were the three misfits, as my wife liked to call them. Part of Jon's story ends this chapter, his team mate Bob was another great 800 runner that I coached, and their friend Steve was one of our best. Steve Lumbar was an individual champion at the Swain Invitational in Duluth and he finished 4th in both the Minnesota State Cross Country Meet and the 1600 of the Minnesota State Track Meet. The day he won the Swain Invite I found him about 15 minutes before the race, rocking out to loud music in the school van. He was alone, lying in the back, and the music was very loud. I debated about talking to him and getting him to the starting line, but I decided to leave him alone. He made it to the line just fine, and he was the fastest cross country runner out of about 300 runners on the course that day. He was a smooth runner, he has and had a great smile, and he is still a dear friend. After a brief stint at Kansas where there were a few academic problems, Steve came back to Minnesota. He spun his wheels for a bit but he has now established a fun, productive life in St. Cloud, Minnesota. He let me know that he is actually teaching others in his job one day a month, and somehow he and I had a good laugh about that. He does a nice job of keeping track of my teams and my individual running. He does a great job of being a husband and a father.

Many of my best runners for boys seem to have come in groups of 2. Leif Larsen and Pete Miller were two of the best. They were part of that 7:58 3200 meter relay team mentioned in Mile 13.1... Leif went on to run for Missoula, Montana and had a very successful tenure there. He felt he should have been allowed to redshirt his senior year and take a full fledged attempt at Olympic Trials, but the coach didn't allow that. Pete ran for the University of North Dakota and followed that up with a brilliant road racing career. He became one of the top runners in Minnesota and even finished very high as one of the top Americans at both Twin Cities and Grandma's Marathons. He also served as president of the Minnesota Distance Running Association and he currently co-directs a running blog that covers many aspects of Minnesota running.

There have been some high level achievements coming out of our program. I could share so many stories, but the joy and honor is to know that so many student athletes learned that success is possible. They knew that what they believed in and how hard they worked would bring about positive results. They knew that many people will be successful and rise to the top, and if they were willing to commit to their goals and continue to work at them they could be a part of that group. They also knew that it was important to be happy and feel good while you were making all of this happen. Our approach, our manner in how we attempt to do our best, is really what is most important. Everyone wasn't a national champion, everyone didn't place in the state tournament, and everyone didn't win races. Hopefully everyone did believe in themselves, try their hardest, and accept what they were able to achieve.

Laura was a very peripheral team member. She should have been a varsity runner, but with her poor attendance and her lack of consistency it just didn't happen. Many years later she lives in the Twin Cities, a mother of 3, and now she runs just about every day. The seed was planted, and running is a significant part of who Laura is as an adult in society.

Ben still says I was one of the two most influential people in his life. He jumps out of helicopters. He is a rescue worker for the Coast Guard. His work schedule revolves around either jumping into snow covered terrain or icy cold water. He was actually a double or back up for the young trainee person training as a rescuer in the movie "The Guardian", starring Kevin Costner. Evidently the movie is very realistic because that is how they train and some of the actual footage in the movie is Ben and his crew on the job. His learning how to run, and work hard, and being the best athlete he can be, has resulted in his qualifying for one of the most demanding jobs anyone could have. That testing record board that ends their training does have Ben's name on it. He still holds the record for the mile run! Wow, what an honor to know the impact that his involvement in Cross Country and Track had on his life. All the way to the extent that when he has down time from his job he also participates in triathlons and running races.

They call, they e-mail, they stop in, and yes they even show up at the starting line of races. They get married, sometimes to each other, they have babies, and they become contributing members of adult society. I am just proud that many of our former runners still value a life built around doing their best and in many cases, keeping the quality of their lives on a higher level through running. One special friend, who for over a decade was also a business partner, is the subject of the final writing for this chapter. Jon defeated one of the best runners in the state to have a great day and qualify for state by getting second place in our regional competition. He wasn't college bound, he was an excellent leader, and he still runs today. As captain his senior year he was a huge part of our success. We were actually ranked as high as second in the state during his last season, going into the state meet we were ranked 4th. I lost my third runner to a pulled hamstring because he tried so hard in the finishing kick at regions. (That runner is now a licensed attorney and has a great corporate job near the Twin Cities.) Jon didn't make it to the finish line on the State Meet day I have chosen to describe. I think he hyperventilated. He said it felt like a bear was squeezing him and he just couldn't get any air. The team still finished 9nth in the state without my second and third best runners, and Jon and I met that day in the middle of the University of Minnesota Golf Course.

"I HUGGED A CHILD TODAY"

It was one of those times when nothing else mattered.
Being a man of direction there was something I had to do.

The crowd was to the south, I headed north.
He came walking, back in a slump, sparkle gone from his eyes.

Total devastation, ultimately humbled, mega bummed.
One of those times when words are hardest to find.
The next thing I knew we were on the ground, him sitting,
Me hugging and all the emotion emptying out.
As the vessel poured out and emptied I was so
much in touch with my life and what it was all about,
that I knew this was where I was meant to be.

We went for a walk then, two men, headed south.

**Lesson learned: The personal impact you can have on someone's future
is very hard to predict. Being there, supporting, shaping, and believing can
be extremely rewarding.**

WHY DO WE RUN?

ANOTHER FAVORITE MANTRA,
"...I WILL RUN AND NOT GET WEARY..."

January 23, 2003

I had about two minutes left to the finish of the 5k. The wind was on my back, the sun was shining, and I just wanted to check the watch. I looked down as it changed to twenty-one minutes. Not bad for a winter run in the ice and snow. I finished hard, stopped my watch. No one caught me in the kick and that good old feeling of crossing the finish line was once again enjoyed. I ran through the finish area, bent over a bit, and brought my hand up to check my time. Not one number was showing on my watch! A total blank screen. I had dressed just right for the temperature, four below with a negative twenty-two degree windchill. My body had felt good. Lower arms and hands were a little chilly at the start, but they felt fine once we were into the race. One hundred and forty people showed up that day. The race was called the Polar Days 5k, and my normally functioning watch was simply too cold to work. (My first thought might be that I had a bad battery, but it was a new watch and it worked fine the day before and for many days after the race.) Makes you wonder what the human body is capable of if a person is crazy enough to set their mind to it.

A friend once asked, "How come I never see you smile when you run?"

How does a person get out almost every day, in any kind of weather, and still enjoy this thing called running? Now, we don't wear a huge grin when we are out pounding the pavement, but I guess the most honest answer is that we are smiling on the inside. I knew a young female runner who always did smile when she ran, even when she was racing, and honestly, that was a little too weird. The "game face", the stoic gaze, or just the usual old far-off detached looks are more common. Then again, when was the last time you thought about how your face looked when you were out for a run? We usually have more important thoughts weighing upon our minds, like that sore hamstring, our running route, or our speed for that day.

My mind loves it when I take it for a run. I have admitted many times that I am psychologically addicted to running. I think that is a good thing. I often wonder what long term effects years of running will have on my knees and my hips. At the same time I see the continued benefit to other parts of my body, and I sincerely hope the benefits over shadow the ill effects. More important than the physical effects is how my mind is affected by what I do. Running truly brings me a happiness I cannot compare to anything else. Oh, there are other things that bring me joy, but the feeling that comes after a good run is just special. I don't know how else to justify or understand why I began running over forty years ago, and why I woke up and went for a four mile run the day I was writing this.

There have been lapses in my running calendar, but I think the longest non-running span in that entire time is the first nine months after I completed college. Things had been intense for four years, and I just didn't care to run for a while. When my teaching and coaching position started, it was just a completely natural thing for me to get back on the roads. My head was ready to get back to where it really did belong. Since I had been doing some lazy, unhealthy, fun things with my life, it was time to change that. One by-product of that time period was the extra weight I had accumulated from the old German source of entertainment -all those beers that I like. Even that I can see in a positive way, because when I started putting in the miles I was given the privilege of experiencing "shin splints" for the only time in my life. Having competed against and trained with people who had dealt with this injury, and later coached student/athletes who were affected by them, it was a good learning experience for me. Pain, aspirin, and water therapy seemed to get me through it. Being stubborn, taking responsibility for what I had done to myself, and making new goals for myself got me past that point in my life. Once I lost a few pounds, iced many times, stretched and bathed my legs to a healthy place, the pain disappeared and never returned.

After healing from my shin splint problem, I got serious about my running and that was when I headed toward that 1979 Boston Marathon. Somehow, the sum total of high school running, college running, and running with the athletes I coach resulted in a love for repeating that simple task that puts me in a place where I know I want to be. That phenomenon continues, day after day, week after week, month after month, and even year after year. The day before I wrote this section I skied for an hour and a half through the beautiful, pristine, snow covered trees of northern Minnesota, and loved the feeling of an endurance workout. I was just out there, totally content, not concerned at all with how those precious moments of life, that all of us plan to use in so many different ways, was being spent. The steady breathing, the increased heart rate responding to the demands, the mind driving the body along the trail moved me through an enjoyable workout. The culminating feeling has become of prime importance to me. It has helped me get out of bed in the morning and often drives me towards the next goal. It helps my life feel more complete.

I like to think I approach life in a very balanced and healthy way. Maybe it goes back to being involved in both music and athletics for my last years of high school and my first years of college. Running in college at an average of twelve miles a day and spending about five hours a day with my music was just not working. That became way too stressful for me and it resulted in a very negative existence for a short period of time. Once I dealt with a few things and got myself back to a better place, life improved. But always, and still, the running continued. The running has always made more sense to me and when I dropped the music major, my running began to improve. The decision was definitely right for me, and has allowed me to experience and achieve much success.

Running just seems to naturally bring different things into my life. Another business partner, as well as the one I mentioned earlier, came into my life because of running. We run together, we sweat, we train, we race, we visit, and then if things seem right, things may go to a higher level. My next door neighbor was the same way. He talked to me about my running. He slowly started to experience a few steps down the road, and all of a sudden we were doing one of my favorite six miles loops together.

Forcing the joy of running on anyone would never work. Asking my students to run laps or being not so surprised when they choose to run laps, does get things going. As a coach, I try to make life on the run available by modeling how my own running program is part of a healthy lifestyle. Making life on the run available, or showing by example what many years of running means to me as a person, conveys there is something happening that is worth noticing. If the person happens to want to share in the actual doing, all the better. It also provides company and positive feedback to perpetuate my personal reasons for what I am doing.

My personal best times are a thing of the past. I still dream, I still wonder how fast I can be over a given distance. At fifty-seven years of age I have centered on the fact that I think being active is important. For the past four years I have organized my life around a goal of completing three miles worth of physical work for every day of my life. I keep track on my "Runner's World" calendar, and I monitor my progress. The majority of my work has been actual running, and I have come to the conclusion that nine minutes of running time is equivalent to a mile. Every day of the year, my goal is to attain an average of three miles. If I miss a week, I am twenty-one miles behind. For some that may seem easy, for others it may seem a little crazy. It works for me because I've always had motivation to maintain that level of fitness. I have heard it said, the most difficult step out the door is the first one. Honestly, most days that is not a problem because I just love getting out and being active. The formula also includes biking, kayaking on the Mississippi River, canoeing, working the treadmill and elliptical, and even weight training time. I just convert whatever exercise effort I do to an equivalent amount of mileage. It seems to work well and I like the results.

This "formula" seems to allow for a workable balance for my life. My wife and I have joined the same exercise club, so we spend some time together doing a variety of things to make up our workouts. When I cross country ski with friends after work, we get to spend time together away from the work site, enjoy each other, and I continue to log the miles. My coaching philosophy has always included active time together with the athletes. During the season, gaining mileage towards my desired total of 1,095 miles for the year was quite easy. You might think going to visit family or going on vacation would provide for some off days for maintaining mileage. That could be true, but I almost always run when I am on actual vacations. I sort of see it as research. Running becomes a great way to discover things about the place you are visiting. Where are the good restaurants, the park or museum you want to visit later in the day? It also goes back to that thing of just needing to run, especially after maybe some long time sitting in an airplane or driving in the car. The body and the mind are usually ready for that run. Many of those runs are repeat positive experiences at relatives or repeat vacation spots. For example, years ago I had a goal I am still hoping to accomplish, make it to the top of "Harney Peak" in the Black Hills of South Dakota.

How long will my life as a runner continue? I really don't know. My knee and my one hip have started to be a bit of an aggravation. It is one of those things, like many I have experienced over the years, that I hope goes away. Beyond that, I still have many things I would love to experience. My neighbor's medal from the Disney Marathon did look like something I wouldn't mind having. Whatever the future brings for me, it won't change the importance or the benefits of running. I have always lived life wondering what is behind the closed door or around the next corner, so who knows where the next run will take me.

I do live on the not so mighty Mississippi River. It is small, clean and it can be a very refreshing summer place to take a dip. It is also wild and natural. Many of you might see it as a large creek or stream. It meanders, causing motor boats to have a tough time because it is so shallow, and it runs continuously. Even on this winter day, at temperatures below zero, it looks to be frozen solid, but I wouldn't try to cross it because the current keeps parts of it open. I love where I live and it seems to have a powerful calming effect on me when I need it. Life on the run and life on the river has been very interesting. I like what the following poem says to me.

"ADVICE FROM A RIVER"

GO WITH THE FLOW
IMMERSE YOURSELF IN NATURE
SLOW DOWN AND MEANDER
GO AROUND THE OBSTACLES
BE THOUGHTFUL OF THOSE DOWNSTREAM
STAY CURRENT
THE BEAUTY IS IN THE JOURNEY
YOUR TRUE NATURE.

(author unknown)

If you have heard and read about some things in this book that may appeal to you, I will spend the rest of my life promoting running and running well. I have worked with both guys and gals and I feel very comfortable coaching anything from the 800 to the marathon. My home phone number is 218-751-7611, e-mail is dbartz@paulbunyan.net, and I would be willing to help you identify and fulfill your dreams.

Coach Dennis "Barny" Bartz

Lesson learned: A running life has taught me to value life on the run. I live it that way most days of my life, and my life is very comfortable because of it. Yours can be too!

TRAINING FOR ROCHESTER, MINNESOTA, MED CITIES MARATHON

The third week in January of 2007, I was sitting in my recliner, and the telephone rang. It was our daughter, "Hello, Dad, how ya doing?"

After a brief visit she went on to say, "Oh really, been running a little huh? That's great. By the way, I think we should do a spring marathon."

Oh boy, this was just too much like that same phone call I had made to my parents thirty-six years ago. It was like "Mile 1" all over again. The only difference here was I knew exactly what we were getting in to, and she wouldn't be running the marathon alone. We would be doing it together. I wasn't sure what that really meant, but more important now was which spring marathon we would enter. The reason she was calling now was dead-lines were approaching.

My mind went back to two years earlier when I had wanted to run the Rochester Med Cities Marathon. My training was well on the way to heading to southern Minnesota for another marathon in our state that I had not run. It was three weeks out and I was running a half marathon just south of the Twin Cities. Things were going well on the rural route on county tarred roads through a farming community. We were about ten miles into it, the weather had cooled to the upper forties, and it had been raining for the past two miles. I was making a nice forward move on a couple of racers on a medium sized hill when a good looking lady runner came cruising by me. I had decided that I had given up enough spots for that day, and I was going to stay with her. She was wearing yellow shorts and a white top, and I convinced myself I would not be letting her get any further ahead. I followed her back to the outskirts of the small town, New Prague, and decided to make a move and go past her.

I pulled up, using a slight acceleration, and as I made it about one stride past her, I experienced instant and total muscle lock up. My right calf wanted to stop and it wanted to stop now! I did stop, I limped, I jogged, I had the form of an eighty-five year old person with a bad limp, and I clumsily finished the race.

I struggled through a maddening week and accepted the inevitable: I would not be running the marathon in three weeks. Along with the training and the planning, this collection of writings was supposed to be concluded along with that 2005 Rochester Marathon. Somehow it had been shelved, slowed down but not forgotten, and left to be finished.

"No seriously dad, which marathon should we do?"

Well, we needed to look at the possibilities. We were very familiar with Grandma's Marathon, and their sign up deadline was coming. I had done the Fargo Marathon, the other local spring option that has a short portion in Moorhead, Minnesota the previous spring, and then there was Rochester. I simply said that was the one that I wanted to do the most, and we agreed that would be our goal. It was going to be held on Memorial Day weekend, and we had four months and one week to prepare.

Our daughter, Traci, lived in St. Paul at the time, and as I have mentioned, she had run the Twin Cities Marathon. That was her only marathon experience so far, but it had been very positive, and her time was four hours and ten minutes. My near-disaster marathon in Fargo the previous spring had resulted in three hours and thirty-eight minutes. So, how were we going to approach doing twenty-six miles together? We left that to be figured out later.

January worked out to be fifty-eight miles for the month and ended with my wife and I going to Las Vegas for a week. During the month I had run a mile race and a mile relay in the college alumni race, as well as a 22:05 winter 5k, and as a result, my right hamstring was a little stressed. I hoped the vacation would be a smart time to rest it and spend time with my wife, son and daughter-in-law.

The first part of February finished up with our Vegas trip, and then I started to train with more regularity. I can get scientific in a hurry. I can also get bored. Most of this book has been about personal experiences and feelings about myself as a runner. I hope it has demonstrated a love for running. However, there has been a whole lot more going on than just how we feel about running. I have many numbers and figures and even two different kinds of heart rate monitors to give me enough data to fill another whole book.

One February workout shows how I approach things. Out of boredom and needing to look outside at the weather rather that going out and facing it, I hit an interval workout on the elliptical trainer. After ten easy minutes of gradual speeding up, I decided to hit a two minutes on, two minutes off series of hard and easy. I went through eighteen cycles and arrived at a stride rate of

150 strides per minute during the active rest time and 190+ stride rate during the hard two minutes. This resulted in my heart rate coming down to close to 115 beats per minute during the rest phase and generally about 135 during the work time. The workout ended up to be a very satisfying morning spent at the fitness center. My highest heart rate was 147 beats per minute which is about 88% of my maximum, and the repetitive 135 beats per minute were a little over 80% effort. I felt that was a good effort for thirty-six minutes of hard working time and I followed it with some abdominal work, a short stationary bike ride, and twenty-one minutes on the treadmill at 8:56 minutes per mile pace. I equated the whole workout to eleven miles of running and it was my biggest volume workout so far as I approached the Rochester race in May. Basically, I had three months to go.

My last two weeks of February were twenty-nine and thirty-one miles, so I was starting to average over four miles a day and improve my conditioning. The most interesting run of the month was a nine-miler in St. Paul with Traci. We were at my in-laws for the weekend and had planned for a Saturday morning run. She was a little late getting her day started, but she came over to her Grandparent's house at about ten o'clock and we headed out the door. Not far from their house is a new boulevard where the traffic is quiet, and there is a nice wide sidewalk. After about a mile the walkway dips down into a valley, leaves the roadside, and gave us some shelter from the winter wind. We were running with snow all around us, but the path was clear. As we went under two bridges, we came to the end of the trail. Further on there was still a trail, but it was not tarred and not totally clear. Traci, always being one for adventure, suggested we try following the new trail. We eventually came to a nice portion that simply had two black, gravel wheel tracks going between two sets of railroad tracks. We were about six and a half miles into the run, and just moving along at a nice pace. All of a sudden, our serene experience of a quiet, enjoyable winter run was interrupted by an obtrusive, loud, and obnoxious siren!

We were being pulled over by St. Paul's finest while we were running! The man pulled up to us, and sat in his squad car talking to us. He did ask what we were doing and then his second sentence was, "You aren't terrorists, are you?" I had a smart comment in mind, and I later learned my daughter did too, but we said no, we were just out on a training run. Evidently we were supposed to give him our names and a warrant was mentioned; then he let us continue our jog back to Grandma's house. However, he did make us go back the way we came and told us how to get back to a main road we knew. It seemed we were on railroad property, and it was supposed to be off limits to all pedestrians, including runners getting ready for a marathon. We told others the story when we rejoined our family, and had a good laugh over the whole thing.

I decided my March goal should be a five mile a day average. Knowing

I had a week of spring break away from work, I had plans to spend the time accomplishing some nice miles. I wanted to get a feel for how my conditioning was coming along so I planned two ten miles runs in forty-eight hours. The roads had become clear of ice and snow, which made a huge difference as to whether or not I would run outside, and as to how far I would run. The first ten miler was done on a loop from our home since I knew the distance and the route. It was a clear, late winter day with a slight breeze and about thirty-five degrees. My light gloves didn't last very long, and I wore a thin stocking cap and my windproof running suit. The miles came easy and I was right on for 8:30 pace for the first three miles and ended up a little slower pace later in the run. It was easy, it didn't seem taxing, and my right hamstring was a little tight, but not bad.

Two days later, it was a similar day with not much wind. I was staying at a time-share a few miles north of Brainerd, Minnesota, and I found a nice, curvy, county tarred road that went through a wooded area. I started on my run and after running a little over three miles, I saw a different road heading north that was a Minnesota State Forest road; I decided to make a change and take that. The trees were thicker, and of course, they were leafless in March in Minnesota, and I headed back into the forest. The road had more curves and several rolling hills, and it was really enjoyable. As I stopped for a personal nature call, I became aware of the many critters awake in the woods that morning. There was a woodpecker drumming, a crow cawing, and several other birds singing. The run continued on to an area with cabins by a lake, and then came to a fork in the road. I was at forty-three minutes of a planned forty-five minutes out, and I decided to turn left. I came to a small, iced over area near the end of the road and stopped to turn around. I looked down to my right and saw a cabin sign that read, "Almost Heaven". I don't know if I was that close, but I was enjoying a good run and headed back to the resort. I ran the second half back faster, enjoying the new pair of Reeboks I was wearing for the first time. The entire run had gone well, and I felt I was getting stronger and my mileage was improving.

I reached fifty-four miles that week and the month ended at 159 miles, making my goal of five miles per day, my longest run being thirteen miles. I felt my training schedule was going well. One thought that seemed significant was that my four longer runs had been done in three different pairs of shoes. I found myself wondering which pair would make the most sense to wear for the upcoming marathon.

The second weekend in April brought Traci home for Easter. We planned a sixteen mile run for Easter Saturday, but the morning arrived with temperatures in the thirties and with a terrible north wind. Rather than fighting winds higher than twenty miles an hour, we asked our loyal wife and mother to give us a ride north of town on a county road that I knew. We did a one way run, all with the wind, as we ran back to our house. I suppose some would say that was silly, but it really made sense to us for that day. Traci had actually worn three shirts, but had two tied around her for most of the run. As long as we were facing the sun and had the wind on our backs, the run was quite comfortable. We covered the sixteen miles with very few problems, and it was a good training run for us. It took us two hours and twenty-eight minutes, but it was a good confidence builder.

Then it was time for some racing and more planning. We decided to do the St. Cloud half marathon on April twenty-first. There was actually a ten kilometer race an hour from home the week before, so I decided to do that. It was a first time race and the field wasn't too intense. As a matter of fact, I had the lead with three other people for the first mile. One person dropped off, and after about ten minutes my other two fellow racers went on ahead. I decided their pace was a little too aggressive and came through the first 5k loop at twenty-two minutes, then continued on in the same place throughout the rest of the race. I finished third overall, first for my age group, and ran 45:20. It wasn't a great time, but a good strong training run that gave me confidence for the up-coming half marathon.

The next weekend, the two of us headed to St. Cloud from our opposite directions. We had signed up for the race together, but we planned not to run together. Training had been going well, and this was one of those races where I had problems in the past. The previous attempt my calf had cramped up, so I wanted to do well and have a positive experience. We met in St. Cloud at the motel on Friday night and went to Ciatti's Italian restaurant for our pasta fix. The night went fine, but we had an abbreviated night of sleep as we were awakened early by a loud, long thunderstorm. We headed over to the college for the start of the race in my daughter's car. We already had our numbers and timing chips from the night before, so we just needed a short warm-up and stretch time. There were some incredibly ridiculous bathroom lines in the field house, so we headed up the stairs to the locker room area and that proved to be much more efficient. I went back outside for a short jog, came back indoors to finish drinking my "Amp," complete my stretching, and my relaxation exercises. The relaxation techniques that I like to use before a race I had learned in a class as part of my masters program. This class had also taken place at this same facility, St. Cloud State, in the 1980's.

The two of us jogged back to her car, made our final decisions about race clothing, and approached the starting line. I was wearing a short sleeved, throw away t-shirt, and a moisture wicking racing shirt. The previous rain had stopped, and Traci hoped we could at least start the race with no rain. That didn't happen, as we left her car it began to drizzle. I gave Traci a hug behind the starting line, and told her that if it went well I would see her at the finish line afterwards. I also said if it didn't go well I would see her somewhere on the course. I headed over to the port-a-pot line and was surprised to see one part of the tree trunk ahead of me was still dry. I leaned against that and stretched out my calves and Achilles tendons, and decided not to wait in line for the bathroom. I went back to the start line, about ten people deep from the front and checked out the day's comrades. I saw a former high school athlete on the other side of the street, went over and greeted him, and came back to my favorite right side of the street.

Many key events of my life have been precluded with the Star Spangled Banner, so even though it was a surprise, I continued to get my brain set for the day as those very familiar words and musical phrases echoed through the campus on that April morning. The next loud noise was that of the starting gun, and we began our thirteen mile tour of St. Cloud, Minnesota.

The extra shirt was tossed before I even reached the first mile in 6:54. That seemed a little fast, and I followed that with a 7:20 for the next mile; then I settled in to a more relaxed pace. I did a misstep going around a corner right after the four mile mark and my right foot gave me the first scare of the day. It only bothered me for a few minutes, and once we got to the flatter, smoother street it seemed fine. I kept telling myself to keep it conservative, not over stride, and keep it healthy. When I tried to accelerate and take longer, faster steps my hamstring and other things seemed to give me negative feedback. I made it to the nine mile mark where I had the problem three years ago, and had even more determination to do the next mile in a healthy way. It went so much better this time, as I took the turn to the final recreational trail and I headed to the finish line. I was surprised I hadn't been able to pass people the last three miles, it was a strong racing field. The finish felt very good, my pace remained constant, and it was a very positive finish.

My hamstring had held up, I crossed the finish line at 1:37, averaging under 7:30 per mile. I went back to where my wife was cheering, greeted her, and kept jogging backward on the course to find Traci. It took a little longer that I thought, but after watching quite a few runners, there she was. I was happy for her, she looked like she had come thirteen miles after getting drenched by the rain and I knew she was ready to be done. She made it to the finish even though one of her feet was really bothering her. Her time was 1:50 and we were both happy we had reached this level. We had six weeks to go. At this point going twice that distance for the eventual marathon seemed a little crazy, but we would leave that for our heads to deal with at a later date.

I finished the month of April, again averaging five miles per day, with long runs of sixteen, thirteen, eleven, and fourteen miles. The eleven and fourteen mile runs were the Friday and Saturday a week after St. Cloud. This is my favorite training method of convincing myself that I am ready for 26 miles. I like it better than doing a twenty or twenty-two mile continuous long run like many other marathon training plans suggest. Friday afternoon I went out and ran the fourteen miles. It came really easy and there was no doubt I was going to make the distance. I took about an eighteen hour break between the runs, most of which was sleep time, hydration, and some good carbohydrates. The next morning I ran five and one half miles out and back to my house. Running a total of twenty-five miles in about twenty hours, helped me know that if all things went well I would make the marathon one month later. The right hamstring continued to be an area I needed to treat carefully. I never reached the point where I went in for a massage, but I did soak in the bath tub a few times and did a lot of stretching. My April weekly mileages had added up to thirty-four, twenty-seven, thirty-five, and forty-two miles. There were still four weeks of training to go, and the last two months had continued to help me feel very confident.

During the time of our training for the Rochester Marathon, Traci's life course had taken on a new direction. She was approved and granted a graduate stipend to further her collegiate studies the next fall in Seattle, Washington. Her studies would be furthered in the area of Biological Statistics and she would be moving to Seattle in the fall. For that reason and others, I committed to running the marathon with her. The plan became to run from the beginning to the end as a father/daughter tandem.

As we began the month of May, Traci had a busy schedule. Having more time and feeling like my running was going well, I decided to do the Minnewaska 30k race that first weekend. The race was located a couple of hours northwest of the Twin Cities and they were offering cash prizes for the different age groups. I had done thirty kilometer races before, and they had taken a lot out of me. I knew I needed to approach it cautiously so as to not ruin my chances for the upcoming marathon, but I felt my preparation was adequate. Figuring our marathon pace would be a little slower because we were running it together, I decided to do the Minnewaska race aggressively and run as fast as I could.

Every race plan may need to be adjusted on the actual race day. Race day for the Minnewaska race arrived with a very strong southeast wind. The race course went counter clockwise around a lake, and I knew the wind would be on our backs early. I also knew there would be one terrible stretch into the wind, and it would be four miles long. We took off on our trek around the lake, and I found myself at the two mile mark at 14:10. I was behind two excellent, young female runners that I knew, and decided this was a little too aggressive, and I intentionally backed off. I threw my racing shirt to a person I knew, and began enjoying the fifty degree temperatures and the act of repeating mile after mile. I was virtually running alone from that two mile decision until I was approaching the turn going into the four miles of wind. I looked back and three people were closing on me as I got closer to the turn. I made my turn from the bike trail to the high, wide, windy stretch of tarred road going through a farming area. The wind was very strong! One of the chasers caught me within a half mile of the corner. We talked a bit and I asked if he wanted to share the wind. We ended up taking turns leading for three telephone poles while the other person drafted. The wind was swirling so much, that it sometimes didn't even help to follow somebody. It did make it easier mentally, if not physically, and we continued to take turns that way for all four miles of wind.

At the eight mile mark the race course took a left turn, the wind becoming much less of a factor, and I met my wife at the planned spot. I drank some more of my power drink and asked her for my small strip of terry cloth I like to carry for wiping sweat, then I got back to business. My wind partner really took off, and I did the same as we went down closer to the lake in a sheltered area and continued to make our way around. I came to the half marathon in 1:42, just five minutes slower than I had raced that distance two weeks earlier, and I felt fine. My time at sixteen miles was 2:06 and I continued on to the finish in 2:28. I finished sixteenth overall and had won my age group. That was a very pleasant surprise, because they awarded $300 for my efforts. More importantly I had come through a nice 18.5 miles and I felt very prepared for the upcoming marathon.

Traci had felt I had over trained one year earlier for the Fargo Marathon, so I forced myself to approach the rest of the month in a very conservative fashion. I really felt I had enough miles behind me, and with three weeks to go the most important thing was to get enough rest. I worked out four times in the next week for a total of eighteen miles. Part of that easy mileage week was personal, as our youngest child graduated from college, and I needed to take care of the things that went along with that. The second week out I also ran four times, but two of the workouts were twelve and ten mile runs, for a total of thirty-one miles. The week before the race I ran twice, a six mile run on Tuesday and five miles on Friday. With my three days of protein and three days of carbohydrates, I hoped I was ready for another marathon starting line.

Lesson learned: Family is very important, and we need to fine time and ways to enjoy them.

26

O   O

FATHER/DAUGHTER ROCHESTER MED CITIES MARATHON, 2007

Marathon weekend finally arrived. Sometimes the waiting gets a little crazy. Doubts may start to enter your mind, and you just want to get on with things. The ride to Rochester, Minnesota, home of the world famous Mayo Clinic, would take us at least six hours of total driving time. I left home Friday evening with a support crew of my wife and son. After four hours of driving, we stayed with relatives in St. Paul, and then picked up Traci at about one o'clock on Saturday. We hit pasta at "Noodles" in the Twin Cities, then drove down to my niece's home west of Rochester. I had emailed her and her husband, they had researched the course, and they knew the area well. They drove us around and showed us much of the route that we would be running the next day. The hills from the town of Byron where the race would start into Rochester seemed significant, but other than that everything looked great. The county road connecting the two towns had gentle hills that kind of rolled through the beautiful farming country. As we entered Rochester we went by the fire station where my niece's husband worked and then started the actual tour of Rochester. They took us to the "Running Room" in Rochester to pick up our race packets, and everything became official. Our numbers and our timing chips were in our hands.

It was great to see someone who had presented me with an award for finishing a marathon 36 years earlier. Mr. Jeff Galloway was the featured guest at the "Running Room." I waited in line to greet him and share that I had been at this for all these years. I also told him about the writing of this book and that the weekend would be helping me write the ending. He was happy for me, appeared very fit, and I was pleased to be able to visit with him on this significant weekend in my life. Month after month I have read his advice in Runner's World, as well as some articles he had written over the years, and it seemed like a lot of things were coming full circle. Here we were staying in the home of my oldest niece, and the next morning I would be running a marathon with one of my children. An important running celebrity that had once presented me with a running trophy so long ago, had joined us in Minnesota on a racing weekend.

Dinner that evening was a near disaster. Trying to carbo-load, we went to an authentic Italian restaurant in downtown Rochester called "Victoria's." Everything about it seemed great; we were seated right away, I allowed myself one relaxed glass of Chardonnay which I drank with my salad and several excellent pieces of bread, as well as about four glasses of water. Then the food came. It all looked exquisite and scrumptious, except for mine. I had what most resembled a huge burrito with marinara sauce all around it. I cut into it and there was not one noodle or one vegetable in sight. I could not help but react with surprise because this was not what I had ordered! The server knew something was wrong, I voiced my concern about what I had been served, and she left to do something else. While she was gone I asked our group if they minded if I waited for a different meal. When she came back, I asked to see a menu and pointed out to her what I had actually ordered. They were very gracious, replaced my meal, didn't charge me for my food, and brought me the biggest plate of angel hair noodles and vegetables that I had ever eaten. My meal was fantastic, and with all of the bread I had consumed, I couldn't even quite finish all of it. I was definitely carbo-loaded. My personal marathon math for three days of carbohydrates was preserved.

We headed to my nieces home for relaxation, watched the Minnesota Twins lose an extra inning baseball game and went to bed about ten. Our hosts got us up at the planned time of ten minutes after six. Traci had some cereal while I consumed a Cliff Bar and my large can of Amp. When we arrived at the school in Byron where the race began, we stepped out of the vehicle aware that the wind was definitely blowing. The race would be starting on a hill and the temperature was about forty-four degrees. We decided to use the twenty-five minutes remaining prior to the race to scope out the field, the facility, stretch, and use the bathroom. When we went to the locker room to use the facilities, the women's line was, of course, three times as long as the men's. Being psyched and moving fast, I did my thing and found my daughter a different bathroom with a much shorter line. Little did I know, the one I found was a one-person facility, so actually her line still didn't move very fast. I stretched, drank some more, and began to check my watch with an increased amount of anxiety because at the start of Traci's first marathon, she had been in the port-a-pot when the gun went off. I knew she did not want to be in that same place for the start of her second marathon. Thankfully, we did get to the starting line with about three minutes to spare, and we were set. I had chosen to wear a long sleeved, old throw-away shirt, a short sleeved throw-away, and a moisture-wicking sleeveless racing shirt.

new golf course. On this pleasant sun-shiny morning, we hugged and lined up about twelve rows of people back from the start. Traci thought that was too far up, but I felt comfortable there since we had committed to running together. The starting commands were given and as the gun fired into the morning air we began our first 26 mile run together. I was very happy to be in this place, at this time, with my daughter. After about a mile I threw away the long sleeved shirt. The throw away short sleeved shirt lasted until nearly the two mile mark. The first two and a half miles were a loop in the small town of Byron, Minnesota. From there we crossed the highway going south, and then began running on the old road that was parallel to the highway, traveling east into Rochester. I totally missed seeing the mile split, the two mile split, and the three mile split marker which is not normal for me. The excitement of the day must have been doing strange things to me. Traci had caught the three mile marker, and informed me we were just over eight minutes a mile, and she was fine with that. Finally at four miles, I easily saw the four mile red flag with white letters about four feet up in the air. I have no idea how I missed the first three markers, but I felt fine that we were pacing along about 8:10 per mile.

From mile three to mile ten we were going towards the sun, wind on our backs, rolling through the country, and clicking off very close to eight minute miles. Mile seven was actually under eight minutes because we had the favorable wind plus a long downhill. The hills proved to be very do-able and gradual. They appeared not to take a lot out of us, and we were going over them easier than quite a few of the people around us. That was one reason I wasn't afraid to line up at the start quite near the front: I had researched the field and it didn't look to be extremely competitive. The sunglasses felt great, but we were heating up just a little. I would guess the temperature was in the low fifties by now, wind still on our backs, and sunny. At mile eight our support vehicle pulled up along side us, and we both gave our shirts to them. Traci was now running in her jog bra and I was down to no shirt. That was perfect. I did have my small piece of torn wash cloth to wipe off sweat so it wouldn't cause burning in my eyes which I find very uncomfortable. We ran by my nephew's fire station, had considered using it for a bathroom stop, but it was on the wrong side of a busy road. We kept pushing to the ten mile drink and bathroom stop. Traci had been needing a pit stop, so I stretched while she used the out house. I also drank a glass of water and brought both of us one more as she was coming out of the port-a-pot door. We had taken 1 hour and 24 minutes to get to this spot and spent two minutes taking care of business. This was very comfortable for both of us.

Our drinking strategy was every other two mile stop we would do water, then Powerade. Traci had some energy packets with her, but I figured I had consumed enough carbs in the last three days that the drinking would get me through. I guess you would say I am a minimalist and don't like to carry, or wear anything more than is absolutely necessary.

We were now into Rochester proper. The middle portion of the race seemed confusing and not quite what our tour guides had predicted, however, the course markings were well done, and they had many great volunteers doing a good job wherever they were needed. We reached the half way mark at an hour and fifty-three minutes. As the half marathoners headed across their finish line, we began our second half of the marathon. We were both very pleased with our time, knowing that if we could stay somewhat close to our pace, our mutual goal of breaking four hours was certainly in reach.

From there the course went over an out and back southern loop that was almost entirely on tarred trails near the river. It was easy to feel our rhythm and the miles continued to click by methodically. We crept into the upper eight minute range, but tried to keep doing the automatic nine minute calculation and keeping our times below that number. Traci shared some comments about her second marathon being easier than her first, and what a nice day it was. She was being very positive, and we were feeling like our training had been done right. Eventually, she did begin to struggle through a few of the miles and at mile seventeen we had our first one over nine minutes. I could feel when she was dropping the pace or not moving forward to others in the field, but I tried not to push her too hard. I felt we had been plenty aggressive in our early pacing and that things were progressing well. At the same time, she reacted perfectly to a slower mile and applied herself back to the pace to make sure it never happened for two miles in a row. After mile eighteen, we were passed by very few people. Before long we were meeting the eventual winners coming towards us and viewing the field up close and personal as we continued to click through the miles. Some parts of the trail were quick, little rolling pieces that caused some extra pains to the knees and muscles, but they weren't that bad. The trail offered some shade and basically we were running on flat ground. By now we were obviously dealing with some aches and pains, but overall, it was a great course.

At twenty miles several people had planned in advance to quit for the day at a special archway, signifying their end of the race. Beyond that we did a short out and back section and then headed back on the same tarred trail toward the finish. I was psyched as we had passed that significant, fictitious, adjusted half-way mark of mine, and there was no doubt we were going to make it. Twenty miles had passed with little difficulty and we were indeed confident about running the last six miles. I told Traci there were two thoughts left for us for the day. The first thought for our focus involved getting back to the mall at the end of the bike trail, and then we would have only a short run left to the finish line. She chose to add a third thought: taking off our shoes. It may sound weird after twenty-one miles, but the mile marks felt like they were coming up quickly and they were a welcomed mark to reach. We were continually catching people, not quickly, but at a nice steady rate. Some people that we were meeting on the outgoing trail seemed to need encouragement. I became quite vocal and greeted several folks. With about three miles to go we met a group of twelve people running out together. When we were quite close to them, I yelled, "Hey, let's party!" It seemed like they were already having a great version of their own private party. Soon after that we met a quite elderly man who was not dressed in his running finest, and he looked way too old to be out on a marathon course. He didn't look that strong and did look quite lonely. However, he was giving it his best, and I assume he made it fine. Seeing him made me really happy I had my daughter by my side.

When we were half a mile from the finish line, I made the age old mistake of looking back. I told Traci there were two people gaining on us, and she made it very clear that she didn't care about them. She had things in perspective: they didn't matter. What did matter was that we were doing what we could do together, and besides, we knew we were solidly under the four hour goal. We kept our pace to the end, and even though one of the other runners did go by, we crossed the finish line together as we ended the Rochester, Minnesota, Med Cities Marathon in three hours and fifty-four minutes. Subtracting the time for bathroom stops, in our minds we had accomplished a very satisfying and very special 3:51 marathon.

Yahoo! We took our shoes off! It did feel good, and all three of our late race goals had been accomplished. Mom, son and niece were on the other side of the fence in no time. As we started to hand our shoes to them our slow functioning, marathon blissful brains remembered our computer chips had to be taken off. I tried a taste of a water bottle, set it down and left it. Water didn't really taste that great at this point. A cold, blue Powerade tasted much better. We made our way out of the runner's area, and after a banana and a bagel, we walked to our group. Traci wanted to keep standing, and I just wanted to get off my feet. It's funny how your individual focus becomes the most important thing at this point. After several minutes of hugs, congratulations, and story sharing, we nimbly walked to our support vehicle.

Our gracious hostess, my niece, and proud wife and mom, wanted to know what we had in mind for the rest of the day. As focused as we had been and as intentional as so many things had been for weeks and months, Traci had the quick answer: she wanted a beer! Maybe she even wanted several. That's my girl. After 540 miles since January first and 26 miles in one day, a glass of beer seemed like the perfect next step. We had joined 312 marathoners, 414 half-marathoners, and 70 relay teams in a nice package of early morning exercise. Our finishes were 108th and 109th, with an 8:56 average pace, and Traci had run her fastest marathon. Wow, we deserved a cold one!

*Finisher's Medal
and T-Shirt*

Some say that running is life. While that may be a bit of a stretch, to me it seems like running is a great metaphor for life. Approach it with a certain degree of optimism, don't be afraid to go for new experiences, and apply yourself as best you can to whatever you attempt. While on the course continue to move to the front, listen to your body and surroundings, and have a definite goal in mind. I had been extremely focused to reach that marathon finish line. Perhaps the biggest motivator being that Traci called and asked me to experience it with her, and I became even more determined that we would be successful. The finishing place and the finishing time were not the greatest thing in the world. For me, the experience became one of the greatest things I have ever accomplished. We had planned and succeeded at something we held to be very significant, and we did it together. What could be more important than that?

Running for your life is not for everyone, but for those who physically can and do find value in it, it can certainly enhance every part of your being. My mind and body are different and better because of the steps I have taken, and yours can be too. Now in a new and different way, beyond the fact that my children have all shown they value a healthy lifestyle, the connection has gone one step further. While our family has often been one in the spirit, and of one mind, my daughter and I have now gone somewhere together on a whole new level. Being a father is one of the greatest blessings that could have ever come my way. Finishing a 26 mile race with Traci was, in a way she can really understand, the ice cream we got to have for dessert.

Run for your life, because you have to, need to, want to. Whatever the reason, if it works for you, just RUN FOR YOUR LIFE!

Lesson re-learned: Running is a great metaphor for life!

26.2

ONE MORE FINISH LINE!

Why do I have a three inch scar on my left knee cap?

If you are still with me, thank you. Either you are a fellow runner who also will never quit, or you are interested enough in my running to make it to the finish line.

I sincerely hope you have learned a little while reading these pages. It is my hope and desire that you can find some encouragement and that you will continue to move your body down the road in a way that makes sense to you. More importantly, may your body and mind continue to be health-filled as you finish that next running route. Along with all that, I have one more story I just need to tell.

My focus is often the next bigger, more important race that I choose to place on my horizon. It works out best for me to select something out there, somewhere, to be my next goal to accomplish. That keeps me motivated, interested, and intentional about what I am doing. Having my constant three miles a day average as part of my daily focus also contributes to getting things done. As a result, I never seem to have any problem getting out on the roads and trails. My running log is almost always with me.

The spring of 2009, some time in early March, I signed up for the Seattle Rock and Roll Marathon. Once again my side-kick of a daughter agreed to sign up right along with me. The race would be held on June twenty-seventh, and since our daughter was in her second year of living in Seattle, it just seemed to make sense to run it.

Time and training were rolling along nicely and the race was two weeks away. It was a Sunday, thirteen days before the race, and my nephew was up visiting from St. Paul. My wife was already out west visiting our daughter and my son and his family in Vancouver, Washington. Dan, my seventeen year old nephew, and I decided to do some work on the land that my partner and I had purchased. We were in the process of clearing trees to make a road into the development.

After showing my nephew the lay of the land, we decided to take down four large trees in one area, followed by clearing out the other side of the area by the main road. Things were moving along well, I had dropped the larger trees, cut them up, and Dan was cleaning up the mess I had created. As I switched over to clearing the smaller brush by taking out several small ten-foot trees, I felt the chain saw snag my pant leg. I told myself to be more cautious and went after the other trees in the area. Looking down I realized there was blood running down my leg! Maybe it was time to stop cutting. I looked down and realized there was quite a cut on my leg because my pants, sock, and shoe were turning blood red.

I immediately shut down the saw and told my nephew I had cut myself. It honestly did not hurt, and I was surprised at the amount of blood. I walked over to my truck, took off my bloodied clothes, and threw on an old pair of running shorts. Seeing a partial roll of toilet tissue in the truck, I decided that would make an appropriate direct compress, and I covered the wound.

We took inventory of the saw and other equipment and got in the truck. I knew I should not drive and Dan found himself in the driver's seat of my eight cylinder Ford F150. He started the engine, put it in gear, spun the tires and slammed on the brakes. It was time to re-evaluate. I told him it was a bigger vehicle than he was used to driving and he would need to take things easier. I also told him I might pass out. I have a lot of training in First Aid and CPR, and I knew about the possibilities of going into shock. I told him the hospital was about seven miles in the direction I was pointing, and he would have to relax and get me there.

Without further incident, we made it to the hospital emergency room. I was dirty, bare footed, partially undressed with red streaks running down my leg. With a stiff legged, bent over walk, I was escorted to the triage area. There I sat. They spoke with me briefly; then I waited for quite some time. Evidently, my toilet paper compress was an acceptable method of dealing with my problem. Eventually they asked for all the information, and I was shown to the emergency room.

The doctor was very concerned and very thorough. Between him and his assistants, they anesthetized, cleansed, and flushed the wound. The doctor also cleaned up my cutting work that I had performed on my knee cap. Evidently an oily chain saw with a jagged cut was not the best way to put a hole in the human body. As he was sewing me up, he informed me of two things. While visiting he knew I had planned to go with a group to the Minnesota Boundary Waters later that evening. He cancelled that trip. He also cancelled my running of the Seattle Marathon. Hearing that, I broke down a bit, put my hands over my eyes, and had a few bad moments. He asked if he was hurting me or what was wrong. I needed to tell him how disappointed I was and how angry I was with myself for having this accident. He more or less said that was just the way things had to be, and I would need to handle it. After thirteen stitches, two prescriptions, and numerous materials to continue cleaning and covering the wound, I was on my way.

Having gotten used to my truck by now, Dan drove me to my house. We discussed plans, I called my friends, and it was decided that Dan would still go with the group on the canoe trip. I understood why I could not make this trip. I have been to the Boundary Waters several times and it is an area where there are no facilities for anything except a throne on a hill for going to the bathroom. There would be no way to keep my knee sterile. On the other hand, I knew Dan would love the experience. He had never had the opportunity to visit the area, and I wanted him to still be able to go.

After he was picked up by my five friends later that day, I was now alone. I was also upset. I finally called my wife and told her what had happened. Her response was, "I don't need to come home, do I?" Well no, there was no reason for that, but after talking to her I had nothing to do but sit and think about what had happened. Across the room, I was looking at my camping gear that, although extremely organized, now would not be used. I looked down at my leg, now being protected by a long off-white covering, and I was not a happy person. The dumbest part of the whole thing was I have protective chaps for preventing such a thing from happening, but they were in my truck fifteen feet away from where I cut myself.

The next Tuesday I had an appointment to have my knee cap checked by a bone specialist. He thought things looked good. He had checked my x-rays and did not see any injury to the bone. He had also been working the ER on the previous Sunday and knew about my upcoming marathon. He told me that if I left the stitches in and followed his caring plan, there should be no reason why I couldn't run the marathon. I actually asked him if I could hug him. I was extremely relieved that running could still be a possibility.

Since I was in the training phase called taper, or organized rest, I was hoping the accident wouldn't totally ruin my chances of finishing the marathon. I followed all the directions, took the antibiotics as scheduled, and rested for three more days. I jogged an easy mile on Friday, and my leg did quite well. There was a small amount of bleeding, but the stitches held and running didn't feel too bad. The next Monday I did a five mile easy run with three nice five minute strideouts. Things continued to heal and looked like they might be okay.

The next significant event happened in St. Paul on the Wednesday I was scheduled to fly out to Seattle. I had a one o'clock flight, so I decided to do a three mile jog from my relatives that morning. After about two easy miles, I came to a slight uphill and my right calf locked up on me! I couldn't even jog back to my vehicle. With a combination of limping, walking, and awkwardly jogging I got to my car. Needless to say I was baffled. What the heck was going on and would this marathon ever happen? I had a history of compulsive problems with my calves, and sometimes it had taken months for them to heal. Since cutting my leg I had not been very active, so now I really did not know what was happening.

With three days to go and problems on both legs, I flew to Seattle. My daughter met me at the airport and with a brief explanation she understood what I was experiencing. She had been having problems of her own and had already decided to switch to the half marathon. Her training had been going great, probably the best ever, when an old foot injury resurfaced and forced her to take quite a long rest. That evening we went out to eat at a nice seafood restaurant she wanted to take me to and we discussed our plan of action. This marathon was a little unique in that they allowed runners to switch from one race to the other up until the night before the marathon. We decided we would rest Thursday and run an easy two miles on Friday. Depending on how that went, I would decide which race to run before we went down to the runner's expo on Friday afternoon.

Final preparation day went well. Finally, something seemed to be working, and my conservative two mile jog went just fine. I did not push it, and I kept my stride very controlled. After that we went to the expo to get our shirts, timing chips, and numbers,

I found something of interest at an exhibitor's booth. They were selling compression socks and since I had decided to go ahead and try running the full marathon, I bought a fifty dollar pair of socks. They were anatomically designed, very constrictive, and they came right up to below the knee cap. My muscles felt very secure, and I decided I should wear those the next day.

Marathon morning finally arrived, and I was actually going to start the Seattle Rock and Roll Marathon. I suppose most people would have thrown in the towel by now, but I was determined to give it my best. Both races started at the same time, so my son gave Traci and me a ride to the starting area where we spent some time together stretching, using the bathroom, and getting final preparations ready. We gave each other a hug, we wished each other good luck, and we headed to our assigned areas to begin the races.

It was another huge race. I couldn't even hear the starting commands, but all at once the masses began to move. I was actually running with thousands of people on the streets of Seattle! After a brief residential phase, we were alongside Lake Washington, and I was constantly listening to my body and trying to do things right. There were a couple of twinges here and there, but as long as I kept my stride a little reserved things were feeling fine. I positioned myself near the 3 hour and 40 minute pace group, just in case things worked out real well.

The road along Lake Washington was beautiful on that early morning run. The temperature was pleasant, and I was very glad to be able to be a part of the race. The socks were working and began to feel very similar to a pair of running tights. Around mile six I disposed of my throw-away shirt. Knowing the weather was predicted to get into the lower sixties, I had worn a shirt that I didn't care about. The portion of the race along the side of the lake continued until we reached the nine mile mark. Along the way I was actually feeling good enough that I was considering the possibilities of qualifying for the Boston Marathon. At my age that would take a 3:35, and I wondered if that might be possible. Perhaps it was really silly to consider such a thing after all I had been through, but it was part of my thinking. The miles were clicking by at about an 8:30 pace, and I continued to be very careful.

Miles ten and eleven involved running on the Expressway of Interstate 90. We were actually running on the floating bridge that takes people across Lake Washington. I had been so concerned with getting my body to the starting line I hadn't done a lot of homework about the race. I asked the runners next to me about the road. They let me know we would be turning around, because this road actually continued all the way to the east coast. We made a u-turn on the bridge and continued to follow I90 towards downtown Seattle. It was rather amazing to be moving our bodies at running speed on a highway that moves thousands of cars a day at speeds a whole lot faster than we were traveling. By now we had passed by a dozen or so musical groups. They did help keep me motivated, the only unpleasant experience being listening to the band stuck playing in the middle of a concrete tunnel. The musical echoes were not that enjoyable. As I approached mile 11, I realized my splits were approaching the nine minute area. Even though I was feeling fine, the reality of running fast enough to qualify for Boston was sliding away.

Ever since the original sign up for the race, I had been aware of one special consideration for running this particular race: my daughter. I knew we would be running by the half marathon finish as we started the second half of the marathon. As we approached the turn off where the half marathoners were leaving the course, my main thought was how our daughter was doing. I was feeling confident about my running and was still excited to continue with the next phase of the run.

The marathon field of runners now headed north. We were again running on a rather major roadway serving that part of Seattle. The road was unique in that the northbound traffic travels directly underneath the southbound traffic. This is the roadway that serves to get people along the wharf side of the city. Being on the lower road provided some extra shade for this portion of the run. We moved through that area of downtown and then came to an older, darker tunnel. The temperature was even cooler as we ran through. Now both lanes of traffic were side by side and we faced a long, gradual uphill that would level out on a high portion of roadway overlooking water on both sides.

Even though this was an out and back section taking us through the next nine miles, I was handling that pretty well. My mind did suggest to me it would be a whole lot easier to just turn around and take a short cut. I was constantly seeing runners going in the other direction on the other side of the road.

Once I made the legal u-turn near mile eighteen and headed back towards the finish, I began to accept the fact that I was really, actually going to make it to the finish line. I was enjoying meeting the many runners who were still heading north, realizing that many people were still behind me. But now I was getting very warm. I was definitely using all of the aid stations, by this time totally consuming the energy drinks to help me continue my efforts. Along this return section, I began to notice lots of people stopping to stretch along the side of the course. Most of these people were stretching their calves. I was very pleased mine were allowing me to continue moving down the road. Perhaps my purchase of the compression socks had been an intelligent decision.

We made it back to the downtown area and had one more section to run. I had handled the half marathoners leaving us the first time we came to downtown. I had dealt with having to go out and back to get to downtown Seattle for the second time. Now the day was even getting warmer and we had to do one more, small out and back before we finished. This final section began with running right by the Qwest field again, where we would be eventually finishing. We were now up on the higher part of the road and running to the south, virtually looking down at where our race would be ending after a few more miles. The out portion of this last loop, although only being about two miles long, did get a little tough on the brain. I just tried to maintain my pace and stay with some of the people around me. We weren't really racing, but rather just trying to finish the work we had chosen to do that day. Finally, I reached the last turn around, and there were just two miles left to the finish. I was still looking forward to people and trying to catch up to them, but my only real positive emotion was that I would be able to make it to the end.

I would learn later that the family did see me a couple of times toward the end. My wife told the crew to look for someone not wearing a shirt with long, funny, orange and white socks. That was what I looked like as I made the final right turn and went down the hill to do the last half mile of the 26 mile race. Once again, I just tried to maintain my running pace and simply enjoy the huge crowd that lined both sides of the road. They had iron gates flanking us continually for the last final section that took me to the long anticipated finish line.

I had been working for a long time, and when I finally crossed the finish line and stopped, I was a bit confused as to what to do next. They gave me my finishers medal, and I spotted some chairs outside of the medical tent. I must have looked somewhat okay because the medical personnel asked me why I was sitting there. His attitude seemed to be that maybe I didn't belong there.

I explained that I was rather exhausted and needed a quiet place to remove my bandage. His demeanor changed significantly when I told him what had happened and that I needed to see if my thirteen stitches were still intact. He helped me check out my knee and congratulated me on my effort and my success. I thanked him and proceeded to follow the tired, happy runners out of the fenced area. My son was waiting at the gate to meet me.

Matt took my shoes, socks, medal and water bottle and led me over to where the family was waiting. We were in the huge parking lot that serves the major sports teams of the Seattle area. I sat down on a blanket on the tar and spent some special time with the family. Traci had done well also. In fact, so well she figured she could have actually done the marathon. Our granddaughter seemed to enjoy watching all the very relaxed people and had a nice big smile for a tired Grandpa. We sat in the sunshine and relaxed for about fifteen minutes before gathering our gear to head to the car.

My body had been through quite a thirteen-day ordeal. It wasn't nearly as serious as many other events in life, but it certainly had been interesting. Seattle's run was a very enjoyable experience. It was one more experience that I wanted to be a part of, and fortunately, it worked out that I was able to complete the race. I ended up running the marathon in three hours and fifty-seven minutes. I was thirtieth in my age group and 816th among the men. My overall place was 1,179 out of 5,656 people who finished the race that day. Seeing those results made me feel very fortunate that all aspects of the race had gone as well as they did. Our daughter finished ahead of over 14,000 runners by getting 1,488th place out of 15,682 runners. It was a great day and we were both pleased with what we were able to accomplish.

What lessons could be taken from this most recent marathon experience? At age fifty-six I will probably need to accept the fact that my marathon times are getting slower. If adversity comes our way, we can certainly decide that it will not have to control everything about out future. Confidence, determination, and a positive attitude can accomplish many things. Sometimes the happenings of life don't make sense, but that doesn't mean we can't get out there and do our best.

Lesson learned: We never need to underestimate what we are capable of. The human body, powered by the human mind, really is a marvelous machine. With a little luck, we can accomplish great things.

COOL DOWN

Many folks have said a certain student is my prodigy, my son, my future stud, whatever. Saturday last the kid wanted to go for a run. He teased, he tantalized, and he suggested 16 miles around Lake Bemidji. I laughed. Sure, let's just go see what happens. We headed north, over the river, then east into the wind. It is winter, 30 degrees, ground is white, wind is blowing. He comments, "Nice breeze, that feels good." We continue on, past a lake, over the river again and are nearing the end of the 6+ mile loop when, he says, "Hey, let's do the four mile loop too!" Uh, are you sure? I'm thinking that I can maybe make it, but it will be a total of more than 9 miles. So, instead of running less than half mile to our house, we headed up the icy, tarred hill and started around the second loop. We made our two right turns and head down the last road as a car approached. I make the comment, "Boy I bet that guy is wondering where the heck we came from." He responds, "That's okay Dad, it's good for people to wonder about things." All in all a great run to share with your own child, and we finished up with ease, even cruising up the last hill to end a good time on the roads. His last statement really took me by surprise: "Dad, some day I am going to set a record running across the country, maybe in 10 or 20 years." Wow, how does a young runner's brain start to think like that? Maybe it all started when he was a baby in a stroller and we took him to a road race. Whatever the reason, whatever the reality, it sure felt good to know his values and desires were in such a positive place. That alone could keep me running, keep me excited, and keep me going for several years. After all you don't run across the USA without a well qualified support team.....

Credibility lies in right, left, right, left, and repeating it many times. For me and for those who are able to choose the running path, it also lies in believing life is better because of running.

(Copies of "Run For Your Life" can be ordered through the author. E-mail or call Dennis Bartz at dbartz@paulbunyan.net or call 218-766-0958.)

The running life continues, I finished 2nd in my age group in a 6k in Portland, Oregon in March of 2011, and on April 16, 2011, I was able to finish 8th overall and win my age group division at the Bemidji Stride Into Spring.

(Running photo on back of book provided by Action Sports International.)

SOME SPECIAL RACES OF A LIFETIME

1971 - December – Atlanta Peach Bowl Marathon, Atlanta, Georgia (2:54:49)

1974 - November – Longest Day Marathon, Brookings, South Dakota (4th, 2:49:37)

1978 - October – City of Lakes Marathon, Minneapolis, Minnesota (169th of 1175) 2:59:08 - Just as planned to Qualify for Boston

1979 - April – Boston Marathon, Boston, Massachusetts (2143rd if 7977) 2:46:15

1984 - October – Twin Cities Marathon, Minneapolis, Mn. 2:50:15

1985 - June – Grandma's Marathon, Duluth, Minnesota (940th of 6243, 3:15:48)

1985 - August – Paavo Nurmi Marathon, Hurley, Wisconsin (Age 32, 3:01) Success after not finishing the same course in '73 and '74

1986 - July – Detroit Lakes, Mn., 10 miler, 62:52

1991 - October – Edmund Fitzgerald, Duluth, Mn., 20k 1:22:05

1993 - June – Grandma's Marathon, Duluth, Mn. 2:54:38 (40 years young)

1993 - July – Bemidji Jaycee's 10k, Bemidji, Minnesota - 2nd, 36:56, Very hot!

1993 - August – ½ Marathon, Mora, Minnesota - 1:25:33 (67th of 599)

1993 - September – Minneapolis, Minnesota Masters 15k Championships, 59:03

1993 - September – Bemidji, Mn., Jackpine Classic 25k - 1:36:51

1995 - October – Kansas City Marathon, 7:15 pace at 3:07:3, 45th of 453

1996 - April – Boston Marathon, 100th Annual, 3:12:4, 5,024 out of 36,000 runners

1998 - June – Grandma's Half Marathon, Duluth, Mn., 1:31:41 (236th out of 3867)

2001 - June – Grandma's Half Marathon, 1:36:37, son 1:39:34, daughter 1:41:44 (315th out of 3787)

2003 - November – ½ Marathon, Bemidji, Mn., 1:41:35

2004 - January – Las Vegas, Nevada, ½ Marathon, 1:32 - 235th out of 2659 runners

2006 - May – Fargo Marathon, Fargo, North Dakota 3:49:30

2007 - May – Rochester, Mn., Med Cities Marathon 3:54:19 WITH DAUGHTER!

2009 - June – Seattle, Wa., Rock and Roll Marathon, 3:57